First World War
and Army of Occupation
War Diary

France, Belgium and Germany

27 DIVISION
80 Infantry Brigade
Princess Patricia's Canadian Light Infantry
4 November 1914 - 31 October 1915

WO95/2262/4

The Naval & Military Press Ltd
www.nmarchive.com
Published in association with The National Archives

Published by

The Naval & Military Press Ltd

Unit 10 Ridgewood Industrial Park,

Uckfield, East Sussex,

TN22 5QE England

Tel: +44 (0) 1825 749494

www.naval-military-press.com

www.nmarchive.com

This diary has been reprinted in facsimile from the original. Any imperfections are inevitably reproduced and the quality may fall short of modern type and cartographic standards.

Contents

Document type	Place/Title	Date From	Date To
Heading	WO95/2262/4		
Heading	27th Division 80th Infy Bde Princess Patricia's Canadian Light Infantry. Nov 1914-Oct 1915 To 3 Canadian Div 7 Can Inf Bde		
Heading	80th Infantry Brigade. 27th Division. (Battn. Disembarked Havre 21.12.14 From England) War Diary Princess Patricia's Canadian Light Infantry. 4th November, 1914, To 29th December 1914		
War Diary	Bustard Camp Salisbury Plain	04/11/1914	15/11/1914
War Diary	Winchester	16/11/1914	22/11/1914
Heading	80th Brigade War Diary of Princess Patricia Canadian Light Infantry Vol I 4.11-29.12.14		
War Diary		25/11/1914	29/11/1914
War Diary	Winchester	01/12/1914	20/12/1914
War Diary	S.S. Cardiganshire	21/12/1914	21/12/1914
War Diary	En Route From Southampton To Havre	21/12/1914	21/12/1914
War Diary	Havre	22/12/1914	22/12/1914
War Diary	In Train en route	23/12/1914	23/12/1914
War Diary	Blaringhem	24/12/1914	31/12/1914
Miscellaneous	Appendices I And II		
Miscellaneous	Princess Patricia Canadian Light Infantry Marching Out State Winchester 20-12-14 Appendix I		
Miscellaneous	Appendix II	21/12/1914	21/12/1914
Miscellaneous	Princess Patricia Canadian Light Infantry	22/12/1914	22/12/1914
Heading	80th Infantry Brigade 27th Division War Diary Princess Patricia's Canadian Light Infantry. January 1915		
War Diary	Blaringhem	01/01/1915	06/01/1915
War Diary	Dickiebusch	06/01/1915	07/01/1915
War Diary	Dickiebusch 252 Corpl W Fry 1284 Lce/Cpl H O Bellinger	08/01/1915	11/01/1915
War Diary	Westoutre	12/01/1915	26/01/1915
War Diary	Dickiebush	27/01/1915	28/01/1915
War Diary	Elzenwalle	29/01/1915	31/01/1915
Miscellaneous	Appendices III IV V VI VII VIII IX		
Operation(al) Order(s)	Operation Order No. 1 By Brigadier-Colonel Non.C.G. Forteacue C.B., C.R.O., D.S.O. Commanding 80th Brigade Area Appendix III	04/01/1915	04/01/1915
Operation(al) Order(s)	Operation Order No 2	05/01/1915	05/01/1915
Miscellaneous	A Form. Messages And Signals		
Map	A Form Messages And Signals		
Miscellaneous	A Form Messages And Signals		
Heading	80th Infantry Brigade. 27th Division. War Diary Princess Patricia's Canadian Light Infantry. February 1915		
War Diary	Dickiebusch	01/02/1915	03/02/1915
War Diary	Shelly Farm	04/02/1915	06/02/1915
War Diary	Heksken	06/02/1915	15/02/1915
War Diary	Dickebush	16/02/1915	21/02/1915
War Diary	Westoutre	22/02/1915	28/02/1915
Miscellaneous	Appendices X XI XII XIII XIV XV		

Miscellaneous	Report On New Area East of St Eloi Appendix X	04/02/1915	04/02/1915
Diagram etc	New Area E of St Eloi Appendix X		
Miscellaneous	Report On General Events Night of 4.2.15 Appendix XI	04/02/1915	04/02/1915
Miscellaneous	Appendix XII		
Diagram etc	Appendix XII A		
Diagram etc	Appendix XIII		
Miscellaneous	Information Regarding German Saps	26/02/1915	26/02/1915
Miscellaneous	Attach On German Sap Appendix XIV	28/02/1915	28/02/1915
Miscellaneous	Appendix XV	28/02/1915	28/02/1915
Miscellaneous	General Plumer Wins Please	28/02/1915	28/02/1915
Miscellaneous	Twenty Eighth Division Wins	28/02/1915	28/02/1915
Heading	80th Infantry Brigade. 27th Division. War Diary Princess Patricia's Canadian Light Infantry. March 1915		
War Diary		01/03/1915	02/03/1915
War Diary	Dickebush	03/03/1915	11/03/1915
War Diary	Westoutre	12/03/1915	15/03/1915
War Diary	Dickiebush	16/03/1915	24/03/1915
War Diary	Poperinghe	25/03/1915	31/03/1915
Miscellaneous	Appendix XVI		
Heading	80th Infantry Brigade. 27th Division. War Diary Princess Patricia's Canadian Light Infantry. April 1915		
War Diary	Poperinghe	01/04/1915	12/04/1915
War Diary	Vlamertinghe	13/04/1915	17/04/1915
War Diary	Ypres	18/04/1915	20/04/1915
War Diary	Polygone Wood	21/04/1915	30/04/1915
Heading	80th Infantry Brigade. 27th Division. War Diary Princess Patricia's Canadian Light Infantry. May (1.5.15-1.6.15) 1915		
War Diary	Polygone Wood	01/05/1915	04/05/1915
War Diary	Bellewarde Lake	04/05/1915	04/05/1915
War Diary	G.H.Q. Line	05/05/1915	06/05/1915
War Diary	Bellewarde Lake	07/05/1915	01/06/1915
Heading	80th Infantry Brigade. 27th Division. War Diary Princess Patricia's Canadian Light Infantry. July 1915		
War Diary		01/07/1915	31/07/1915
Heading	80th Infantry Brigade. 27th Division. War Diary Princess Patricia's Canadian Light Infantry. August 1915		
War Diary		01/08/1915	31/08/1915
Heading	War Diary Month Of August 1915		
Heading	80th Infantry Brigade. 27th Division. War Diary Princess Patricia's Canadian Light Infantry. September 1915		
War Diary	Rest Camp Petit Moulin Farm	01/09/1915	08/09/1915
War Diary	Petit Moulin Farm	09/09/1915	14/09/1915
War Diary	Pradelles	15/09/1915	18/09/1915
War Diary	Mericourt	19/09/1915	19/09/1915
War Diary	Hoissey	20/09/1915	30/09/1915
Heading	80th Infantry Brigade. 27th Division. War Diary Princess Patricia's Canadian Light Infantry. October 1915		
War Diary	In Trenches At Frise	01/10/1915	31/10/1915

27TH DIVISION
80TH INFY BDE

PRINCESS PATRICIA'S
CANADIAN LIGHT INFANTRY.
~~DEC~~ NOV 1914 - OCT 1915

TO 3 CANADIAN DIV
7 CAN INF BDE

80th Infantry Brigade.

27th Division.

(Battn. disembarked Havre 21.12.14 from England)

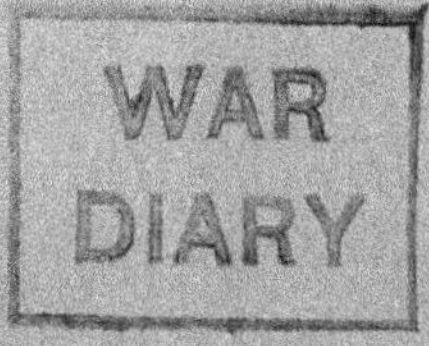

PRINCESS PATRICIA'S CANADIAN LIGHT INFANTRY.

4TH NOVEMBER, 1914, to 29TH DECEMBER 1914.

Attached:

Appendices
I and II.

Army Form C. 2118.

Instructions regarding War Diaries and Intelligence Summaries are contained in F. S. Regs., Part II. and the Staff Manual respectively. Title pages will be prepared in manuscript.

WAR DIARY
or
INTELLIGENCE SUMMARY.
(Erase heading not required.)

Hour, Date, Place	Summary of Events and Information	Remarks and references to Appendices
BUSTARD CAMP SALISBURY PLAIN. 4. 11. 14.	Inspection of Battalion with rest of Canadian Contingent by H M The KING accompanied by H M The Queen, Lord ROBERTS & Lord KITCHENER.	
5 11 14 to 13 11 14.	Bn at Field Training, musketry, digging trenches, route-marching &c.	
14. 11. 14.	Orders received for Bn to move to WINCHESTER	
15. 11 14	Advanced party under Lieutenants FITZGERALD and DE BAY moved to WINCHESTER.	
WINCHESTER 16 11 14	Bn moved to WINCHESTER in 3 trains and camped at MORN HILL	
" 20 11 14.	Bn joined 20th Bde Expeditionary Force other Bns 2nd Bn Shropshire L.I. 3rd & 4th Bns K.R.R.C. & 4th Bn R.B. under Brig Gen Hon. C.G. FORTESCUE. CB. CMG. DSO.	
" 18. 11 14.	Orders to hold Bn in readiness to entrain at 2 hours notice.	
" 22. 11 14.	Emergency duty ready to entrain at 4½ hrs notice from 6 pm until 6 pm 23.11.14. <u>N.B.</u> Essential that preserved rations, biscuit &c should be issued to Battalions on mobilization & held by them ready for a move: none could be issued at WINCHESTER So it was necessary to purchase in order to have one days rations in case of a move.	

5

nil

80th Brigade.

121
4042

War Diary
of
Princess Patricia Canadian Light Infantry

Vol I. 14/1/18.
4.11 — 29.12.14

Army Form C. 2118.

Instructions regarding War Diaries and Intelligence Summaries are contained in F. S. Regs., Part II. and the Staff Manual respectively. Title pages will be prepared in manuscript.

WAR DIARY
or
INTELLIGENCE SUMMARY.
(Erase heading not required.)

Hour, Date, Place	Summary of Events and Information	Remarks and references to Appendices
25. 11. 14	Battalion inspected by Major Gen T. D'O. SNOW Commdg 27th Divn accompanied by Brig Gen HON. C. G. FORTESCUE Commdg 80th Brigade.	
	Bn. on Emergency Duty ready to move at 8½ hours notice.	[illegible]
28. 11. 14	Bn on Emergency Duty ready to move at 8½ hours notice until 6 pm 29th	[illegible]
29. 11. 14	Bn Commenced Musketry Course Selected practices Table B.	[illegible]
		[illegible]

6

(73989) W4141—463. 400,000. 9/14. H.&J.Ltd. Forms/C. 2118/10.

Instructions regarding War Diaries and Intelligence Summaries are contained in F. S. Regs., Part II. and the Staff Manual respectively. Title pages will be prepared in manuscript.

WAR DIARY
or
INTELLIGENCE SUMMARY.
(*Erase heading not required.*)

Army Form C. 2118.

Hour, Date, Place	Summary of Events and Information	Remarks and references to Appendices
WINCHESTER. 1.12.14	Bn on Emergency duty from 6pm until 6pm 2.12.14	HCW
" 4.12.14	Bn took part in Brigade Route march. Very wet.	
	Bn on Emergency duty till 6pm. 5.12.14	HCW
	One or two Coys at musketry daily firing a Course with LEE ENFIELD Rifles issued to the Bn in place of the ROSS RIFLE	HCW
" 7.12.14	Bn on Emergency Duty till 6pm 8.12.14	HCW
" 8.12.14	80th Infy Bde route march via HOSPITAL – CHURCH – TELEGRAPH HILL – LANE END DOWN – Xroads ½ m N. of WHITEFLOOD FM – MORESTEAD – BAREND – CAMP.	HCW
" 10.12.14	Battalion was practised in loading Baggage Wagons	
" 15.12.14	Divisional Route March ITCHEN STOKE – ITCHEN ABBAS – WINCHESTER Owing to both men and wagons being short of establishment, there were many wide gaps	
" 16.12.14	Eightieth Brigade affiliated to following units 1st Brigade R.F.A 1st Wessex Co R.E 83 Field Ambulance	

Instructions regarding War Diaries and Intelligence Summaries are contained in F. S. Regs., Part II. and the Staff Manual respectively. Title pages will be prepared in manuscript.

WAR DIARY
or
INTELLIGENCE SUMMARY.
(Erase heading not required.)

Army Form C. 2118.

Hour, Date, Place	Summary of Events and Information	Remarks and references to Appendices
WINCHESTER 16th 12. 14 (Cont)	27th Division accompanied by H.M. The King accompanied by Lord Kitchener on FARLEY DOWN. Weather fine. His Majesty walked down the line and the Division subsequently defiled past him in column of route.	
WINCHESTER 20 XII 14	8th Brigade left Winchester for Southampton by road. The Battalion which was the third battalion in the line of march, followed the SHROPSHIRE L. I. & left the starting point at the cross roads at 10.15 reaching SOUTHAMPTON DOCKS at 4 p.m. (time later due to checking caused by [illegible] confusion of transport in front of us). Battalion embarked from Berth 46 on CARDIGANSHIRE which already contained the 29th Battery R. F. A. (Major HENDERSON). Embarkation [illegible] hours and ship left at 7 p.m. [illegible] fine	Appendix I ([illegible] State)

Instructions regarding War Diaries and Intelligence Summaries are contained in F. S. Regs., Part II. and the Staff Manual respectively. Title pages will be prepared in manuscript.

WAR DIARY
or
INTELLIGENCE SUMMARY.
(Erase heading not required.)

Army Form C. 2118.

Hour, Date, Place	Summary of Events and Information	Remarks and references to Appendices
S.S. CARDIGANSHIRE 21.XII.14 En route from Southampton to HAVRE	Arrived off HAVRE 5 a.m. Came into dock 1.25 p.m. Commenced disembarkation 2 p.m. Battalion marched off 3 p.m. to No 2 camp, where it arrived at 5.30 p.m. Transport arrived at 8.15 p.m. Showery weather	
22.XII.14 HAVRE	Battalion Route March from 10.30 a.m. to 12.45 p.m. Completed equipment from Ordnance. Ration parties left camp at 4 p.m. Remainder of Battalion at 5.45 p.m. Reached ~~Point~~ Point 3, GARE DES MARCHANDISES ~~[illegible]~~ at 7 p.m. Men in tearing spirits. The whole Battalion had to entrain in one train of 48 trucks. Officers 1, Men 24, Horses 10, VEHICLES 13. Very tight fit, some of the men being unable to sit down. Fatigue parties worked very well. Battalion left at schedule time 11.19 p.m. Showery.	
23.XII.14 In train en route to ST OMER	Reached ABBEVILLE 12.30 p.m. Journey would have been much easier if we had been informed when halts were to be made and for how long	

9

(73989) W4141—463. 400,000. 9/14. H.&J.Ltd. Forms/C. 2118/10.

Army Form C. 2118.

WAR DIARY
or
INTELLIGENCE SUMMARY.
(Erase heading not required.)

Instructions regarding War Diaries and Intelligence Summaries are contained in F. S. Regs., Part II. and the Staff Manual respectively. Title pages will be prepared in manuscript.

Hour, Date, Place	Summary of Events and Information	Remarks and references to Appendices
23.XII.14 (cont)	Reached St OMER 8.20 p.m. Received orders to proceed to ARQUES and to detrain there. Reached ARQUES at 9.40 p.m. Detrainment completed by 12.30 a.m. (24th). The [illegible] for the vehicles were very bad & greatly retarded both the entrainment and detrainment of the Battalion.	Appendix II. Orders for railway journey.
24.XII.14 BLARINGHEM	The guide provided by the R.T.O. confessed after he had gone some miles that he had never been to BLARINGHEM. In consequence it took until 3 a.m. to cover the 7 miles to that village. On arrival at Brigade Headquarters was informed that we were to billet along a stretch of 2 miles, down the road we had come along. The transport pulled off into nearest field & the troops were gradually billeted the last being got in about 6 a.m. Very trying night, after trying day. Fine, cold.	
25.XII.14 BLARINGHEM	Spent morning overhauling packing of transport. Unluckily Christmas comforts not available. Very fine in morning, then misty cold frost.	

Instructions regarding War Diaries and Intelligence Summaries are contained in F. S. Regs., Part II. and the Staff Manual respectively. Title pages will be prepared in manuscript.

WAR DIARY
or
INTELLIGENCE SUMMARY.
(*Erase heading not required.*)

Army Form C. 2118.

Hour, Date, Place	Summary of Events and Information	Remarks and references to Appendices
29.12.14 & 31.12.14 BLARINGHEM	Bn employed with remainder of 80th Brigade in entrenching a line position with support position 200 yds in rear extending from MT CROQUET $\frac{3}{4}$ MILE N E of BLARINGHEM through LA BELLE HOTESSE to STEENBECQUE. Weather wet ground waterlogged & draining of trenches very difficult	[illegible]
29.12.14	Major Gault Capt SMITH & 2 N.C.O.S. went up to trenches of 8th Division at KEMMEL. 24 hours in trenches to learn method of reliefs & gain experience. Valuable hints and information gained.	

(73989) W4141—463. 400,000. 9/14. H.&J.Ltd. Forms/C. 2118/10.

A P P E N D I C E S

I and II

Copy

"Princess Patricia's Canadian Light Infantry. Appendix I

Marching Out State

2

Winchester
20-12-14.

Officers	27
Other Ranks	956
Vehicles	25
Horses	82
Motor bicycles	2
Bicycles	10

Lt. Colonel,
Commanding P.P.C.L.I.

Copy

Appendix II

O. C. — P.P.C.L.I.

1- Please note that the Battalion under your command will entrain as detailed in para. 4 below.

4. Place of entrainment - Gare des Marchandises
Time - 7 p.m.
Date - 22nd December, 1914.

Issued at Havre,
21-12-14.

(Sd.) T. C. Browne,
Major,
D.A.Q.M.G. - Havre Base.

Copy

Princess Patricia's Canadian Light Infantry.

Place	Time due in	Time due out.
Havre	23-12-14.	23-19
Rouen	3.01	4.25
Serqueux	6.48	6.53
Abbeville	12.52	

Havre
22-12-1914.

(Signed) C.E. Birnen,
Capt,
D.A.D.R.T.

80th Infantry Brigade.

27th Division.

WAR DIARY

PRINCESS PATRICIA'S CANADIAN LIGHT INFANTRY.

J A N U A R Y

1 9 1 5

Attached:

Appendices III to IX.

Instructions regarding War Diaries and Intelligence Summaries are contained in F.S. Regs., Part II. and the Staff Manual respectively. Title pages will be prepared in manuscript.

WAR DIARY
or
INTELLIGENCE SUMMARY.
(*Erase heading not required.*)

Army Form C. 2118.

Hour, Date, Place	Summary of Events and Information	Remarks and references to Appendices
1. 1. 15 BLARINGHEM	Brigade inspected by Field Marshal Sir JOHN FRENCH Commander in Chief. Sir JOHN said few words ~~of~~ to the men. Very ~~short~~.	[initials]
2. 1. 15	C.O. & Adjutant went up to trenches of 3rd Division at KEMMEL for 24 hours duty in trenches. Attached 4 ROYAL FUSILIERS.	[initials]
1. 15 to 3. 1. 15 BLARINGHEM	Bn employed on the entrenched position being constructed at BLARINGHEM.	[initials]
5. 1. 15	Marched from BLARINGHEM to METEREN via HAZEBROUCK SYLVESTRE–CHESTRE and FLETRE. Bn formed the Brigade Advanced Guard. Bn much handicapped from want of boots.	[initials] Appendix III Orders for march
6. 1. 15	Marched from METEREN to DICKIEBUSH via BAILLEUL and LOCRE. Lack of boots much felt many men marching with no soles at all to their boots.	[initials] Appendix IV Orders for march
DICKIEBUSH 2.30 pm 6. 1. 15	Arrived DICKIEBUSH and rested till 5 pm. At 4 pm Major HAMILTON GAULT returned to Bn with General instructions with regard to taking over the trenches from the 55th FRENCH Regt 65th Brigade 32nd Division. Bn marched from X roads ½ mi SW of DICKIEBUSH via DICKIEBUSH to road junction ¼ mi NW of VIERSTRAAT.	

(73989) W4141—463. 400,000. 9/14. H.&J.Ltd. Forms/C. 2118/10.

Instructions regarding War Diaries and Intelligence Summaries are contained in F. S. Regs., Part II and the Staff Manual respectively. Title pages will be prepared in manuscript.

WAR DIARY
or
INTELLIGENCE SUMMARY.
(Erase heading not required.)

Army Form C. 2118.

Hour, Date, Place	Summary of Events and Information	Remarks and references to Appendices
	when the Right Half Bn under Major GALLT took over the 2 sections on the right. The Left Half Bn marched to LA BRASSERIE & took over the remaining 2 sections. Time was lost owing to no guides having been provided by the French. Taking over completed at midnight without incident. Line held by the Bn extended 1150 yds as per attached sketch. Trenches were found to be in a very waterlogged condition, no traverses & few dug outs. Distance from GERMAN LINE 40 yds on our LEFT, 200 YDS on our RIGHT. Work of bringing up ammunition to scale of 250 rds per rifle as well as rations continuing till 3 a.m. 7.1.15.	[illegible] Appendix V SKETCH
7.1.15 RICKEBUSCH	Enemy shelled trenches with Shrapnell & H.E. at 9 a.m. & 4 p.m. [Report for day attached] casualties 3 slight.	Appendix VI Daily Report
8.1.15 RICKIEBUSCH	No 4 Coy shelled heavily during early morning. Casualties Captain D.O.C. Newton and 5 men wounded: 2 men killed †. Relieved in trenches by 3rd Bn K.R.R. No 3 & 2 Coys returned to billets in RICKEBUSCH. No 1 to a position in support at VIERSTRAAT, No 4 ditto at LA BRASSERIE. Relief completed 1.30 am 10.1.15. Very wet.	[illegible] Appendix VII Daily Report
251 Cpl W FRY 1284 L/Cpl H O BELLINGER		
9.1.15	Captain Newton died of wounds. Party of Officers & N.C.Os 81st Bde reported to inspect trenches previous to their occupying them. 2 R.E. Officers accompanied them	[illegible]

3

(73989) W4141—463. 400,000. 9/14. H.&J.Ltd. Forms/C. 2118/10.

Instructions regarding War Diaries and Intelligence Summaries are contained in F. S. Regs., Part II. and the Staff Manual respectively. Title pages will be prepared in manuscript.

WAR DIARY
or
INTELLIGENCE SUMMARY.
(Erase heading not required.)

Army Form C. 2118.

Hour, Date, Place	Summary of Events and Information	Remarks and references to Appendices
9 1 15	2 Coys in Support First day Nothing of note	HWd
10 1 15	Second day in Support. Nothing of note to report No 1 Coy hunted a Sniper from tower near VIERSTRAAT.	HWd
11 1 15	Third day in Support. Heavy Shelling by Enemy; 2 or 3 Shells through No 1 billet. Relieved at 10 pm by HQ & 2 Coys Royal Irish Regt Marched independently to WESTOUTRE to billets Arrived 2 30 am 12 1 15	HWd
12 1 15.	Day of rest.	
WESTOUTRE 13 1 15.	Marched 3 pm to DICKIEBUSCH. Went into billets at MILLE KRUISSE. Bn in support.	HWd
14 1 15	Marched at 5 pm and relieved 4th Bn KRRC in close support No 4 Coy at CHATEAU at KRUISSTRAATHOEK HQ No 2 and 3 Coys at ELZONWALLE No 1 Coy at LA BRASSERIE Relief completed about 8 pm Searched Chateau at ELZONWALLE for Spies without result.	HWd
15 1 15	ELZONWALLE pretty heavily shelled during the day. 1 man hit on Shin by Splinter. Marched at 6 pm and relieved 4th KRR in trenches at ST ELOI. Projected attack on GERMAN Saphead by parties from both Battalions postponed. Relief completed about midnight.	HWd

(73989) W4141—463. 400,000. 9/14. H.&J.Ltd. Forms/C. 2118/10.

Instructions regarding War Diaries and Intelligence Summaries are contained in F.S. Regs., Part II. and the Staff Manual respectively. Title pages will be prepared in manuscript.

WAR DIARY
or
INTELLIGENCE SUMMARY.
(*Erase heading not required.*)

Army Form C. 2118.

Hour, Date, Place	Summary of Events and Information	Remarks and references to Appendices
16. 1. 15.	Trenches in bad order, parapets not bullet proof and few loopholes. Relieved by ARGYLL & SUTHERLAND HIGHLANDERS. Relief completed about 10 pm. Casualties killed {No 658 Pte N. McLEOD and No 858 Private H. McNISH} wounded 4 {Pte THORBURN serious, the other 3 slight}. Marched to billets at MILLEKRUISSE.	[illegible] Appendix VIII Sketch of Trenches
17. 1. 15.	Relieved at MILLEKRUISSE by Royal Scots, marched to billets at WESTOUTRE. Settled in billets by 9 pm	[illegible]
WESTOUTRE 18. 1. 15 to 23. 1. 15	In billets at WESTOUTRE.	[illegible]
23. 1. 15 4.30 pm	Marched to DICKEBUSCH and billeted	
24. 1. 15	Marched to VOORMEZEELE and took over trenches at ST ELOI Section C. 3 to C. 10 from LEINSTER Regt. Heavy fire [illegible] during relief. Casualties killed Lieut C. H. PRICE and [illegible] PEPPER wounded four. Trench mortar in [illegible] C 6 [illegible] causing further casualties four wounded. Three officers [illegible] 2nd [illegible] trench C 9 during the night. Weather fine, clear bright night [illegible] difficult	[illegible]
25. 1. 15	[illegible] [illegible] occupied by [illegible] heavily shelled during morning, [illegible] for 17 Germans [illegible] [illegible] [illegible] East of St Eloi. Casualties [illegible] wounded	

(73989) W4141—463. 400,000. 9/14. H.&J.Ltd. Forms/C. 2118/10.

Instructions regarding War Diaries and Intelligence Summaries are contained in F. S. Regs., Part II. and the Staff Manual respectively. Title pages will be prepared in manuscript.

WAR DIARY
or
INTELLIGENCE SUMMARY.
(Erase heading not required.)

Army Form C. 2118.

Hour, Date, Place	Summary of Events and Information	Remarks and references to Appendices
26.1.15	Germans quiet along front. Relieved at night by Royal Irish [illegible] [illegible] from [illegible] Corps. Also [illegible] Casualties Killed Captain S. G. FITZGERALD 730 Private H. WHEALEHAN 1172 Private [illegible] NICHOLSON 740 Private MURPHY 1532 Private CROOK. Wounded Lieut STANLEY-JONES and five others. Marched to DICKIEBUSH and billeted.	Appendix IV No [illegible] Report on ST ELOI Section
DICKIEBUSH 27.1.15	In billets at DICKIEBUSH	
28.1.15	5.30 pm marched to relieve ARGYLL & SUTHERLANDS in support. No 1 & 2 Coys in close support at ST ELOI. No 3 at BRASSERIE. No 4 at Chateau KRUISTRAATHOEK. HQ at ELZONWALLE.	
ELZONWALLE 29.1.15	No 4 moved to form HQ at ELZONWALLE. About midnight heavy firing heard on left of ST ELOI section. HQ No 3 & 4 Coys & 2 Coys A & S Highlanders turned out & marched under C.O. (Lt Col FARQUHAR) to VOORMEZEELE. All quiet & returned to ELZONWALLE.	
6 pm 30.1.15	Marched to ST ELOI and relieved 4th Bn K R R being relieved at ELZONWALLE by A & S Highlanders.	
31.1.15	Relieved at ST ELOI by 3rd Bn K R R by [illegible] Returned to billets at DICKEBUSH. All quiet along the line.	

A P P E N D I C E S

III
IV
V
VI
VII
VIII
IX

Appendix III

Copy No. 9

OPERATION ORDER No.1
by
Brigadier-General Hon. C.G.Fortescue C.B., C.M.G., D.S.O.
Commanding 80th Brigade Area.

7

4th January, 1915.

Reference HAZEBROUCK Map
1/100000

1. The troops as mentioned below will march to-morrow to the area METEREN - CAESTRE - BORRE - MERRIS - where they will billet.
(a) The 27th Divisional Cyclist Company will march to METEREN independently and must be clear of HAZEBROUCK by 10.45 a.m.

(b) <u>1st Column</u>.
Advance Guard. Commander Lt.Col.Farquhar P.P.C.L.I.
1st Wessex Field Co. R.E.
P.P.C.L.I.

<u>Main body in order of march</u>.
Brigade Headquarters.
4th Bn. Rifle Brigade.
3rd K.R.R.C.
4th K.R.R.C.
83rd Field Ambulance.
98 Company A.S.C.

This column will march via SERCUS - HAZEBROUCK - LA BREARDE - CAESTRE - FLETRE - METEREN.

Starting Point road junction immediately N. of E in LE [illegible], to be passed by head of main body at 9.30 a.m.

Units of this column will be billeted as follows -

Brigade Headquarters. 27th Divisional Cyclist Coy. Wessex Field Co. R.E. P.P.C.L.I. 4th Bn. Rifle Brigade.	at METEREN.
3rd K.R.R.C.	at FLETRE.
4th K.R.R.C.	at CAESTRE.
83rd Field Amb. 98 Coy. A.S.C.	at STRAZEELE.

The 83rd Field Ambulance and 98 Coy. A.S.C. will leave the column at HAZEBROUCK and march direct to STRAZEELE.

(c) <u>2nd Column</u>.
Commander Lt.Col.Bridgford, 2nd K.S.L.I.
1st Brigade R.F.A.
2nd K.S.L.I.

This column will march via STEENBECQUE - HAZEBROUCK - PRADELLES to STRAZEELE.

Starting Point cross roads ½ mile N.W. of last E in STEENBECQUE to be passed by head of main body at 10 a.m.

The units of this column will be billeted as follows.

2nd K.S.L.I.	at STRAZEELE.
1st Brigade R.F.A. (less Amm.Column)	at PRADELLES.
1st Brigade Amm. Column.	at BORRE.

2. Baggage and blanket wagons will follow their own units. Supply wagons immediately after refilling will follow the column and will be distributed to the billeting areas under the orders of the Brigade Supply Officer.

3. Reports to head of main body.

[illegible] Major,
Brigade Major, 80th Inf. Brigade.

Copy No.1 Brigadier General Commanding.
2 Brigade Major.
3 Staff Captain.
4 War Diary file.
5 2nd K.S.L.I.
6 3rd K.R.R.C.
7 4th K.R.R.C.
8 4th Rifle Brigade.
9 P.P.C.L.I.
10 1st Wessex Field Co. R.E.
11 83rd Field Ambulance.
12 98 Coy. A.S.C.
13 1st Brigade R.F.A.

Issued by orderly at 6.30pm

PPCLI Appendix IV

Copy No 7

Operation Order No 2
by B. Genl Hutton. C. Fortescue CB. CMG. DSO
5th January 1915

Ref. HAZEBROUCK Map 1/40000

1. The troops as mentioned below will march tomorrow to the road junction ½ mile S.E. of E in DICKEBUSCH.

No 1 Column

Advanced Guard Comdr Major Harrington R.B.
2 Coys 4th Bn Rifle Brigade

Main body in order of march
Brigade Hd Qrs.
4th Bn R.B. less 2 Coys
P.P.C.L.I. less 1 Coy
1st WESSEX Fd Coy R.E.

Rearguard 1 Coy P.P.C.L.I.
Comdr to be detailed by O.C. P.P.C.L.I.

This column will march via BAILLEUL – LOCRE – LA CLYTTE. Starting point road junction of uncoloured road with main BAILLEUL road 1 furlong east of METEREN 10.30 am.

No 2 Column
Comdr Lt Col Fosling 3rd Bn K.R.R.C.
3rd Bn K.R.R.C.
4th Bn K.R.R.C.
will march from FLETRE at 10 am and follow same route [illegible] Column

2. The OC 1st Bgde Ammunition Column will have the head of his Column of S.A.A. wagons at the junction of the BORRE – BAILLEUL METEREN – BAILLEUL roads 1200 yds E of the Starting point at 10.45 am and will move on with the first Column in rear of the 1st WESSEX Coy R.E.

3. The 83rd Field Ambulance will follow the 1st Bde Ammunition Column joining it at STRAZEELE. In the event of the supply of new boots not arriving before the start, OC 83rd F.A. will render all assistance possible in bringing along men who are ineffective from this cause

4. Supply refilling point METEREN CHURCH Sq. Supply and baggage wagons of all units will be taken over by OC 96 Coy A.S.C at the point named in para 2 and will march in rear of No 2 Column in the order of march of units to the same destination

5. Report to METEREN up to 10.30 am after to head of MAINBODY of No 1 Column

J. ? [illegible] Staff Capt
for Brigade Major 80th Bde

NOTICE – A mail will be delivered at refilling point tomorrow morning.

11

Appendix V

SKETCH showing trenches occupied by P.P.C.L.I. from night 6th/7th Jan 15 to night 8th/9th

		Offs	Other
A	1, 2	1	24
	3	1	29
	4, 5	1	40
		1	60 A Section HQ
B	1	Continuous 3	150
C	1, 2	1 NCO	40
	3	1	30
	4, 5	1	12
		1	30 C Section HQ
		1 Rear of Coy	
D	1, 2, 3	3 Platoons line 21 men	
	4	1	21 D Section HQ
	5	Rear of Coy	

Scale about 3" to 1 mile

Grenadier Bois

Bois Quarante

Bois Carre

VIERSTRAAT

from DICKEBUSCH

"A" Form. Army Form C. 2121.

MESSAGES AND SIGNALS. No. of Message

Prefix	Code	m.	Words	Charge	This message is on a/c of:	Recd. at m.
Office of Origin and Service Instructions.			Sent		Service.	Date 12
			At m.			From
			To			By
			By		(Signature of "Franking Officer.")	

TO BRIGADE MAJOR 80th BRIGADE

Appendix VI

Sender's Number	Day of Month	In reply to Number	AAA

P 8 Just returned from inspecting trenches All men are over as then ankles in water Some up to their knees all cheerful AAA Draining impossible until rain stops as ground completely flooded AAA ENEMY shelled trenches with Shrapnel and HE about 9 am 1pm and 4pm fire heavy in places Sixty five? Tech Johnsons in one Section AAA CASUALTIES THREE all slight Shrapnel wounds AAA Machine Guns both damaged by direct hit AAA 12 men in right Section not accounted for they

From

Place

Time

C

The above may be forwarded as now corrected. (Z)

Censor. Signature of Addressor or person authorised to telegraph in his name

* This line should be erased if not required.

58 S. B. Ltd. Wt. W5673/619—50,000. 10/14. Forms C2121/10.

"A" Form. Army Form C. 2121.

MESSAGES AND SIGNALS. No. of Message

Prefix Code m. | Words | Charge | This message is on a/c of: | Recd. at m.
Office of Origin and Service Instructions. | Sent At m. To By | Service. (Signature of "Franking Officer.") | Date From By 13

TO 2

Sender's Number | Day of Month | In reply to Number | AAA

were counted into trench and
are believed to have followed
the French as they marched
out A.A.A. Relief yesterday difficult
as guides supposed to be
provided were not forthcoming
French evacuated one trench NORTH
of VOORMEZEELE - ST ELOI road before
being relieved by Rifle Brigade
I occupied it temporarily to
avoid gap in line but
should be grateful if detachment
could be relieved there AAA Consider
it advisable ~~if~~ for R.E. officer to
inspect trenches with view to draining
AAA PUMPS bailers & TUBS urgently
required AAA HOPE TELEPHONE will

From
Place
Time

The above may be forwarded as now corrected. (Z)

Censor. Signature of Addressor or person authorised to telegraph in his name

* This line should be erased if not required.

MESSAGES AND SIGNALS. No. of Message

Prefix Code m. | Words | Charge | This message is on a/c of: | Recd. at m.
Office of Origin and Service Instructions. | Sent At m. To By | Service. (Signature of "Franking Officer.") | Date From 14 By

TO 3

Sender's Number | Day of Month | In reply to Number | AAA

THROUGH TO MY HEADQUARTERS
TONIGHT IMPORTANT TO COMPLETE IT
TO TRENCHES AAA T[illegible] R.A.
officer could OBSERVE with advantage
from my Headquarters AAA Names
of Casualties SS JACOBS No 1058
C. BIRT No 1361 R. MAGEE

From O C PPCLI
Place BOIS CARRE
Time 10 p m

The above may be forwarded as now corrected. (Z)

Censor. Signature of Addressor or person authorised to telegraph in his name

* This line should be erased if not required.

"A" Form. Army Form C. 2121.

MESSAGES AND SIGNALS.

No. of Message

Prefix Code m. Words Charge
Office of Origin and Service Instructions.
Sent At m. To By
This message is on a/c of: Service.
(Signature of "Franking Officer.")
Recd. at m. Date 15 From By

TO Brigade Major
80th Brigade

Appendix VII (1)

Sender's Number	Day of Month	In reply to Number	AAA
P 10	8/1/15		

One company shelled early morning, considerable sniping in evening. Casualties as far as known as follows Killed No 252 Corporal W. FRY Wounded No 1636 Pte W. A. H. A'COURT severe 65 Pte G. GILBEY slight 75 J. H. FRY slight Officer Captain D.O.C. NEWTON severe AAA Relief by 3rd KRR proceeding AAA Work last night at revetments which are improved Trenches still full of water and conditions trying

From O.C. P.P.C.L.I.
Place La BRASSERIE
Time 10.5 pm

The above may be forwarded as now corrected. (Z)
Censor. Signature of Addressor or person authorised to telegraph in his name
* This line should be erased if not required.

"A" Form. Army Form C. 2121.

MESSAGES AND SIGNALS.

No. of Message

Prefix Code m. Words Charge
Office of Origin and Service Instructions.
Sent At m. To By
This message is on a/c of: Service.
(Signature of "Franking Officer.")
Recd. at Date From 16 By

TO BRIGADE MAJOR
80 BRIGADE (2)

Sender's Number	Day of Month	In reply to Number	AAA
P 13	9/1/15		

Add to yesterday's casualties Killed No 1284 Lce Corporal H. G. BELLINGER Wounded 1049 BUGLER H. BAYLISS No 2 Company SERGEANT MAJOR S. M. BRADLEY ~~AAA~~ No 1656 Pte J GRAY

From O C P.P.C.L.I.
Place VIERSTRAAT
Time 4.15 pm

The above may be forwarded as now corrected. (Z)
Censor. Signature of Addressor or person authorised to telegraph in his name

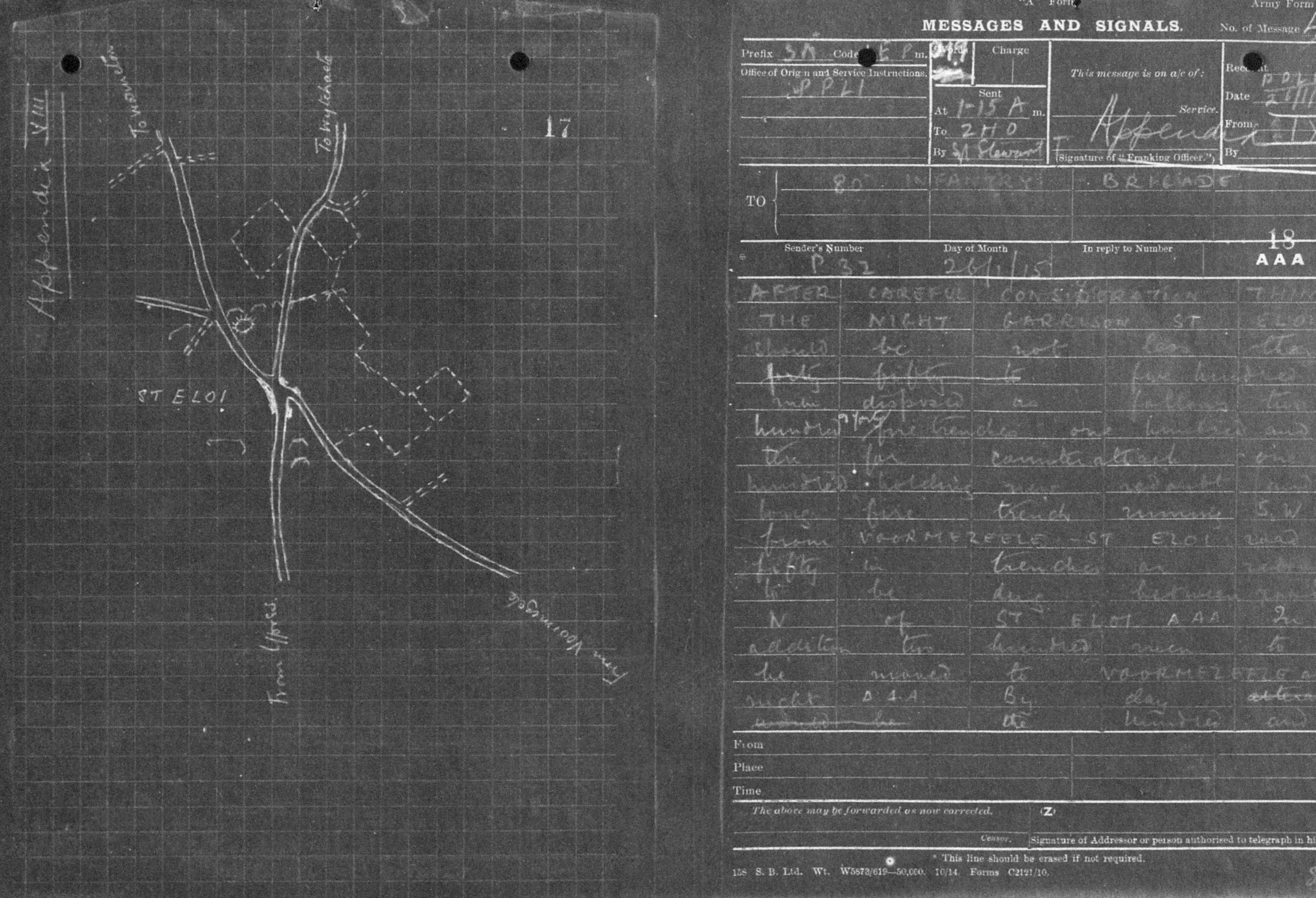

"A" Form. Army Form C. 2121.

MESSAGES AND SIGNALS. No. of Message 42

Prefix SA Code EP m. Charge

Office of Origin and Service Instructions. PPLI

Sent At 1-15 A m. To 2 HQ By [illegible]

This message is on a/c of: Appendix Service.

(Signature of "Franking Officer.")

Recd. at [illegible] m. Date 26/1/15 From [illegible] By

TO 80 INFANTRY BRIGADE

Sender's Number	Day of Month	In reply to Number	AAA
P 32	26/1/15		

18

AFTER CAREFUL CONSIDERATION I THINK THE NIGHT GARRISON ST ELOI should be not less than ~~forty fifty to~~ five hundred men disposed as follows two hundred forty fire trenches one hundred and ten for counter attack one hundred holding new redoubt and [illegible] fire trench running S.W from VOORMEZEELE - ST ELOI road fifty in trenches [illegible] to be dug between [illegible] N of ST ELOI AAA In addition two hundred men to be moved to VOORMEZEELE at night AAA By day ~~alteration~~ ~~would be~~ the hundred and

From

Place

Time

The above may be forwarded as now corrected. (Z)

Censor. Signature of Addressor or person authorised to telegraph in his name

* This line should be erased if not required.

158 S. B. Ltd. Wt. W5873/619—50,000. 10/14. Forms C2121/10.

87

"A" Form.

MESSAGES AND SIGNALS.

No. of Message 4

Prefix	Code	m.	Words	Charge	This message is on a/c of:	Recd. at PPLI m.
Office of Origin and Service Instructions.			Sent		Service.	Date 26/1/15
			At m.			From
			To			By
			By		(Signature of "Franking Officer.")	

TO 2 19

Sender's Number	Day of Month	In reply to Number	AAA

fifty men occupying new trenches and reports could be kept in VOORMEZEELE which would be sufficient as garrison for these place AAA The SAP HEAD at opposite No 9 trench is supported by 3 successive lines of trenches all said to be occupied the nearest being within 20 yards of sap head AAA This makes it impossible to rush sap head without attacking also taking trenches Solution appears to be either to take these trenches or to guide German attack into channel favouring heavy counter from us preferably

From

Place

Time

The above may be forwarded as now corrected. (Z)

Censor. Signature of Addressor or person authorised to telegraph in his name

* This line should be erased if not required.

158 S. B. Ltd. Wt. W5673/619—50,000. 10/14. Forms C2121/10.

"A" Form.

MESSAGES AND SIGNALS.

No. of Message 5

Prefix	Code	m.	Words	Charge	This message is on a/c of:	Recd. at PPLI m.
Office of Origin and Service Instructions.			Sent		Service.	Date 26/1/15
			At m.			From
			To			By
			By		(Signature of "Franking Officer.")	

TO 3 20

Sender's Number	Day of Month	In reply to Number	AAA

from our left flank in neighbourhood C 11 AAA Will take O C LEINSTERS carefully over ground on his arrival here tonight and will advise him to bring the 200 men of VOORMEZEELE under garrison to S P 10 during the night [illegible] Kaiser's birthday of 26/27 and 27/28

From O C PPCLI

Place VOORMEZEELE

Time 12.20 [illegible]

The above may be forwarded as now corrected. (Z)

Censor. Signature of Addressor or person authorised to telegraph in his name

* This line should be erased if not required.

80th Infantry Brigade.

27th Division.

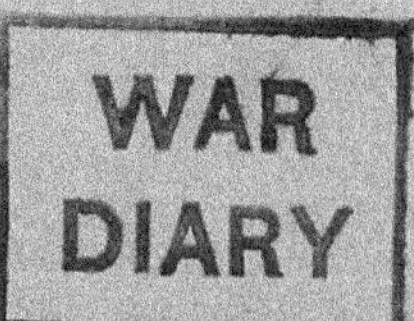

PRINCESS PATRICIA'S CANADIAN LIGHT INFANTRY.

F E B R U A R Y

1 9 1 5

Attached:

Appendices X to XV.

Instructions regarding War Diaries and Intelligence Summaries are contained in F. S. Regs., Part II. and the Staff Manual respectively. Title pages will be prepared in manuscript.

WAR DIARY
or
INTELLIGENCE SUMMARY.
(*Erase heading not required.*)

Army Form C. 2118.

Hour, Date, Place	Summary of Events and Information	Remarks and references to Appendices
DICKIEBUSCH 1. 2 15.	Battalion in billets. In evening visited trenches held by the French Regt on left of 27th Div trenches.	HWd
2 2 15	In billets. Again visited same trenches now occupied by YORK & LANCASTER Regt who had taken them over from the French	HWd
3 2 15.	Marched to ST ELOI & took over trenches from York & Lancaster Regt Section D. HQ at SHELLY FARM.	HWd Appendix X. Sketch & report q.v
SHELLEY FARM 4 2 15.	Line pretty quiet by day though some excitement by night.	
6.53 pm	Report that enemy had broken through 28th Div line N. of CANAL Square I 34c & all reliefs postponed.	HWd Appendix XI. General report. q.v
5 2 15.	Relieved by Leinster Regt after quiet day except for fairly heavy shelling of No 2 Coy in trenches D1 & D2 by German trench mortar. Lieut Sullivan wounded marched to DICKIEBUSH into huts arriving about midnight.	HWd
HERSKEN 6. 2. 15 2.45 pm	Marched to billets at HERSKEN. Weather fine	HWd PPCLI
7. 2 15	In billets H.R.H. The Prince of Wales visited the Battalion.	
8. 2. 15	In billets. Total casualties to date. Officers Killed 3 Wounded 2 Other Ranks Killed 20 Wounded 30 Total Killed 23 WOUNDED 32	HWd HWd
HERSKEN. 9. 2 15	In billets Very fine	
10. 2 15	In billets Very fine H.R.H. Prince Arthur of Connaught visited the Battalion	HWd

2

(73989) W4141—463. 400,000. 9/14. H.&J.Ltd. Forms/C. 2118/10.

WAR DIARY
or
INTELLIGENCE SUMMARY.
(*Erase heading not required.*)

Instructions regarding War Diaries and Intelligence Summaries are contained in F. S. Regs., Part II. and the Staff Manual respectively. Title pages will be prepared in manuscript.

Hour, Date, Place	Summary of Events and Information	Remarks and references to Appendices
11 2 15	4 pm Marched to DICKIEBUSH and went into huts.	
12 2 15	Marched at 6 30 pm and took over trenches 1 to 6 S1 & S2 from 4th KRR HQ at BRASSERIE. Lieut MINCHIN & 20 men returned from ROUEN.	RW
13 2 15	In trenches all quiet.	
14 2 15	5 45 pm. Report that Germans had taken trenches 19. 20 21 at St ELOI. Relief postponed. Very dark night cold & wet. About 9 pm outbreak of enemys fire opposite No 2 & 3 trenches.	RW
15 2 15 4 am	Counterattack on 19 20 21 successful. 3rd Bn KRR took prominent part. Very wet & cold.	
	All quiet during day except at noon when enemy shelled trench 6 killing 2 men & wounding 2.	Killed Pte Palmer, McGan [illegible] " Clayton [illegible]
6.30 pm	Relieved by 4th Bn KRR & by 1 Coy 3rd KRR at VIERSRAAT. Marched to billets in DICKEBUSH	
DICKEBUSH 16 2 15	In billets. Very fine.	G.9.C.L.I.
12 noon 17 2 15	Report that 28th Division had lost trenches. Regiment ready to move at short notice. Very wet & cold. Marched at 5.30 pm and relieved 4th KRR trenches as on 12th.	RW
18 2 15	Enemy shelled BRASSERIE at 3 pm. Killed 1 man and wounded three: otherwise all quiet. Cold wind.	Killed Pte MURDOCK RW
19 2 15	Enemy shelled BRASSERIE at 3 pm. No casualties. All quiet along line. 1 man killed and 1 wounded. Cold wind. Relieved at 10 pm by 3rd KRR and by 1 Coy 4th KRR at VIERSTRAAT. Bn returned to DICKEBUSH. Same billets as on 15th.	Killed Pte CAMERON (1163)

8

Instructions regarding War Diaries and Intelligence Summaries are contained in F. S. Regs., Part II. and the Staff Manual respectively. Title pages will be prepared in manuscript.

WAR DIARY
or
INTELLIGENCE SUMMARY.
(Erase heading not required.)

Army Form C. 2118.

Hour, Date, Place	Summary of Events and Information	Remarks and references to Appendices
DICKEBUSH 20 2 15	In billets. Fine but wet afternoon.	P.P.C.L.I.
10 a.m. 21. 2 15	Marched to rest billets in WESTOUTRE.	
WESTOUTRE 22 2 15	In billets. Capt A. A. ADAMSON. Lieut MARTIN and draft of 111 others joined the Bn. Lieut WILMOT + 5 rejoined from Hospital.	Appendix XI. Extract from Sir J French's despatch + telegram from Sir J F. to Prime Minister Canada
23 2 15 / 16	In billets at ~~[illegible]~~ WESTOUTRE	
WESTOUTRE 25 2 15		
4.30 pm 26 2 15	Marched to billets in the huts at DICKIEBUSH.	Appendix XII A. Defences of VOORMEZEELE
27 2 15	Very cold boisterous weather + wind. Marched at 6 30 am relieve Argyll + Sutherland Highlanders in St ELOI Section Trenches 19 to 22. S14 + 15.	
4.30 a.m. 28 2 15	No 4 coy together with Snipers + bomb throwers (under Lieut PAPINEAU) attacked + captured German sap opposite trench 21. Lieut CRABBE led the attack. The sap was demolished + the trench parapet knocked in. The coy withdrew at daybreak. Lieut COLQUHOUN who had previously gone out to make reconnaissance never returned. Casualties 1 Officer missing#. 2 Officers wounded ϕ Other ranks 5 Killed 7 wounded. 2 missing	Appendix XIII. Sketch of German trenches near St ELOI. Appendix XIV Short account of operation. # Lieut COLQUHOUN ϕ Major HAMILTON GAULT Lieut CRABBE. Appendix XV. Telegrams of Congratulation

(73989) W4141—463. 400,000. 9/14. H.&J.Ltd. Forms/C. 2118/10.

A P P E N D I C E S

X
XI
XII → XIIa
XIII
XIV
XV

Report on New Area East of ST ELOI.
4. 2. 15.

General. 1) The trenches were numbered as shown on the sketch before the ground had been seen. As a matter of fact the trenches were in 3 groups 1) A 2) B. 3) E and C. D & F being support trenches and G dug outs.

Peculiarities 2) (a) The 3 fire trenches are not homogeneous but consist of a number of embrasures more or less connected by trench. In certain cases it is impossible to go from one embrasure to another without getting out of the trench.

(b) There are far too many dugouts, many of them against the parapet which greatly weakens fire from the trench.

(c) The general trace makes it necessary to take strenuous precautions to prevent one trench firing into another.

(d). With the exception of A. they are easy to get into, but the communication trenches should be improved.

(e). The enemy's line is more distant than in other sectors ranging from 50 yds on the right to 200 yds on the left (EICKHOF FARM).

3) Trench A. Wet. Very insanitary: parapet either too thin or fallen away.
A good deal was done to remedy the parapet and to drain the trench on the night of 3rd/4th. An R.E. pump has been left there to continue the work.

It is suggested that a new trench should be made as follows

old trench

With a view to this, four saps were begun on 3/4th & it is strongly urged that they be continued and that a trench 2ft 6. deep with a sandbag & earth parapet 2' high be constructed.

An old French communication trench runs parallel to and 30 yards from the right of A. This is believed to be used by the Germans as a listening post & should be occupied by our snipers.

Work to be done. 1) New trench 2). Communication trench 3). Draining

4) Trench B. Most of the Dug outs have been torn down & proper sandbag headcover & loopholes made. This should be carried on & communication improved both laterally & from front to rear

5). Trench C. As in B. Some draining is also required and traverses should be constructed across dangerous gaps.

6). Dug Outs. Many of the French dug outs round the Farm are wet & should be put straight. A new dug out for 20 men was made by us between SHELLEY FM & A.

7). Machine Guns. The French emplacement in A opposite the German gun was abandoned & new emplacements made in B & E as shown. It is not easy to find sites for more guns but with care two more might be placed in A. (new trench). one firing to right & one to left.

8. Entanglements. Patches of knife rests along front of parapet Not very effective nor placed with any idea of finding German attack.

10. Sanitation. A minimum quantity. "A" Trench has a good many French bodies lying in rear of it & some more are probably trodden down in the trench. The Frenchmen buried in the parapet are marked with crosses.

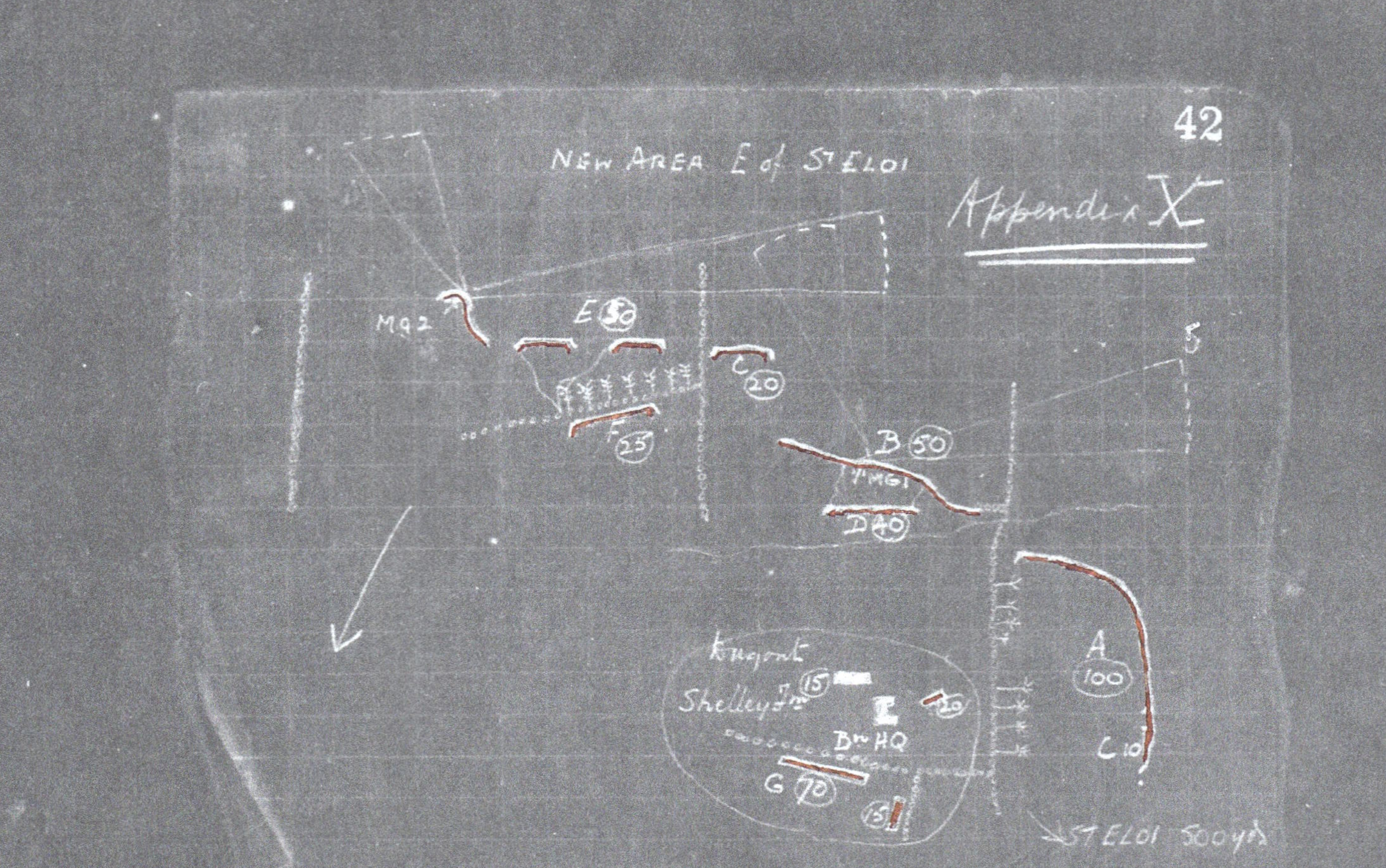
New Area E of St Eloi
Appendix X
MG 2
E 50
C 20
F 25
B 50
MG 1
D 40
A 100
C 10
Shelley's Fm
15
Bn HQ
G 70
15
St Eloi 500 yds

Appendix XI

Report on General Events night of 4 2 15

6.53 pm Enemy reported to have broken through 28th Division N of Canal Square 134C. Counter attack being arranged and all reliefs suspended.

7.55 pm All quiet in our front. KOYLI fairly active on our left. Heavy firing audible on other side of Canal.

9 pm Enemy reported to have occupied a trench immediately next to that held by our left Company who were in danger of being enfiladed.

11.15 pm O.C. Left Coy (Major WARD) reported said trench to be still in possession of 28th Divn Bn holding it being

Lieut COLQUHOUN and 15 men sent to report on situation.

4th Bn K.R.R. sent to SHELLEY FARM to reinforce the Bn.

All very quiet in front.

1.5 pm Lieut COLQUHOUN reported that owing to some misunderstanding certain trenches had been temporarily evacuated on our left. Situation now completely restored normal and quiet.

4th Bn K.R.R returned to DICKIEBUSCH

Result Battalion remained any extra night in trenches as relief was postponed till following evening.

Appendix XII

The following Extract from F.M. Sir John French's despatch of Feby. 2nd is published for the information of the Battn. –

"I may mention in particular the fine appearance presented by the 27th and 28th Divisions, composed principally of Battalions which had come from India. Included in the former Division was the Princess Patricias Royal Canadian Regt. They are a magnificient set of men, and have since done excellent work in the Trenches."

The C. O. wishes to warmly congratulate the Battn. on having received such a compliment from the C in C and is convinced that all ranks will strain every nerve to maintain this high reputation.

Appendix XII 22

Notice

The Commander-in-Chief has received the following message from the Prime Minister of Canada.

"There is but one spirit in Canada, that of resolute determination to force this war to a victorious issue. We trust that the First Canadian Expeditionary Force may soon join the armies and your command and that it will emulate the unsurpassed valour and heroism already displayed often in face of overwhelming odds by the British Expeditionary Forces now in France. We bid you and all the Allied Forces God Speed in your great task.

Signed Bordon."

The Commander-in-Chief has sent the following reply:-

"In the name of the Army under my Command, I thank you for your most kind and encouraging message which has been communicated to the troops. We are full of hope and confidence. Princess Patricias Canadian Regiment has been engaged in the trenches and has fully justified the hopes which their magnificent appearance inspired."

Signed French."

DEFENCES of VOORMEZEELE 11 Appendix XII A

1. Wall 32 loopholes
2. Proposed trench 40x long
3. houses 16 loopholes
4. " 12 "
5. Proposed trench 80x long
6.
7.
8.
9. } Existing trenches

Scale 1" = 150x approx.

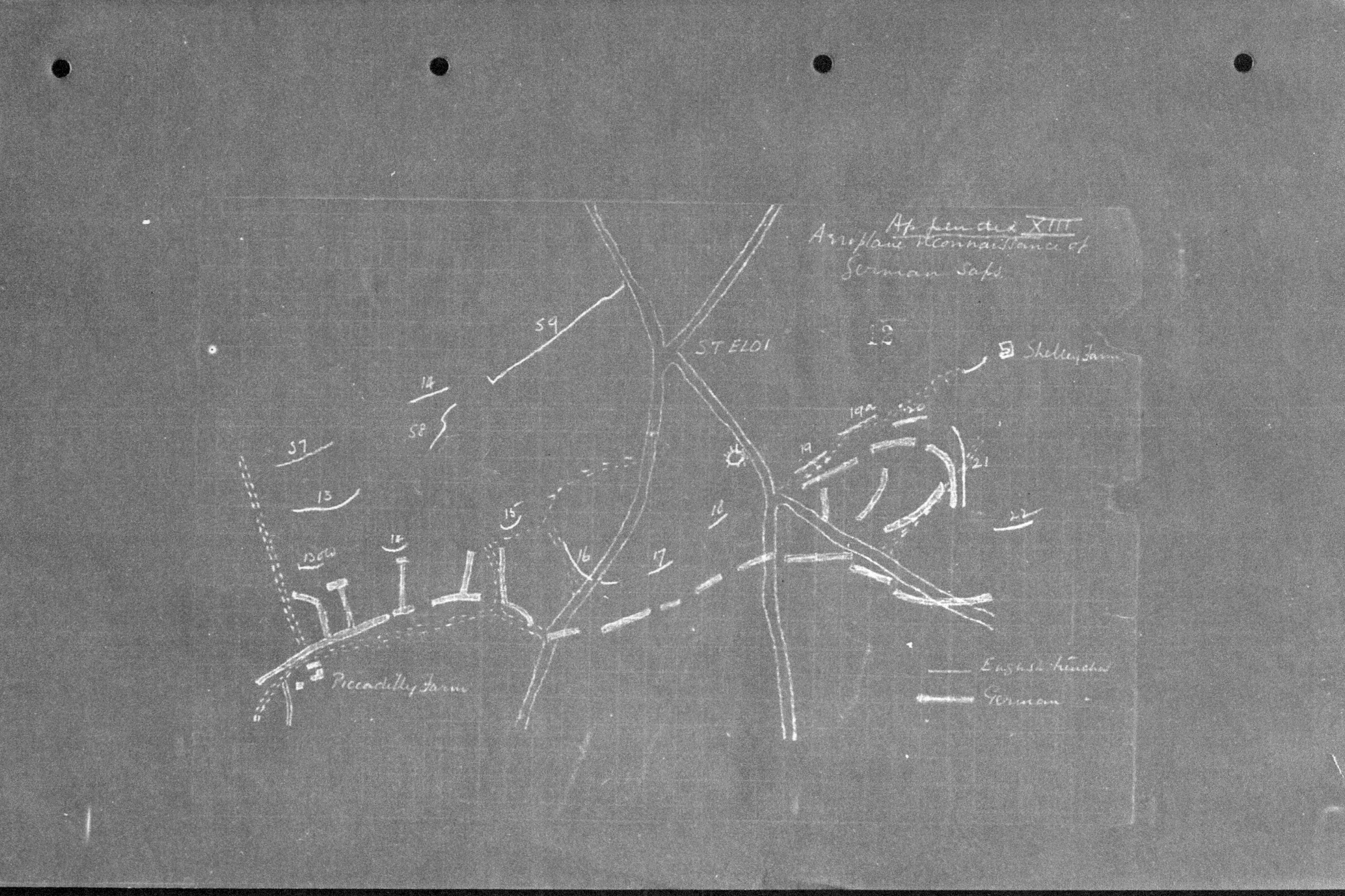

Appendix XIII
Aeroplane Reconnaissance of German Saps.
12
ST ELOI
Shelley Farm
Piccadilly Farm
59
14
58
57
13
13a
18
15
16
17
10
19
19a
20
21
22
English trenches
German

Information regarding German Saps.

1). Opposite trenches 13 to 15
5 Saps. Sapheads start from 5 very conspicuous trees 2 of which are broken.
Sapheads of the two nearest 15 are reported 25 yds & 40 yds distant from right end of 15.

2). Opposite trenches 17 and 18.
Parallels from the original Sapheads & probably others started since have been reported running left to right of 17.
Parallels in front of these two trenches are not continuous & do not yet cover the front of 17.

3). In front of 19 – 21.
These parallels from Saps first reported about 17/18th January are now practically continuous at distances varying from 25 to 30 yds in front of right of 19, 40 to 50 yds in front of 20 & not more than 15 to 25 yds in front of 21.

26.2.15.

Attack on German Sap. 28.2.15.

1 The attack was undertaken with a view to giving a set back to the Enemy who, from the Sap opposite trenches 20 & 21 had become very aggressive & was doing considerable damage to 21 with bombs, etc.

2. No 4 Coy was detailed for the attack & organised as follows: 3 Snipers under Cpl ROSS. – Lieut CRABBE – 3 bomb throwers under Lieut PAPINEAU – Remainder of Snipers – 1 Platoon of No 4 Coy under Sergt PATTERSON – 1 Platoon No 4 in Support – 1 Platoon No 4 with shovels to be ready as soon as trench was captured to demolish the parapet. – 1 Platoon in Reserve.

3. The force was led by Cpl ROSS. from SHELLEY Fm along hedge in front of trench 21 to trench 22, thence to left end of trench 21 which was selected as jumping off point. From this point to the nearest point of German Sap was about 15 yards. The attackers crossed this without difficulty and entered the Sap. Cpl Ross was killed immediately on entering the Sap. Lieut CRABBE then led the Coy down the trench whilst Lieut PAPINEAU ran down the outside of the parapet throwing bombs into the trench. Lieut CRABBE continued down the trench until brought up against a barrier behind which Germans had collected at this point all men except one of the party with Lieut CRABBE were out of action.

In mean time Sgt Pattersons platoon occupied the rear face of Sap to guard against a counterattack, Sgt Major Lloyd & 1 platoon attacked & demolished the parapet for about 30 yds.

After some 20 minutes occupation of the trench combined with work in demolishing the parapet, orders were given for the attackers to withdraw.

The withdrawal was successfully carried out though daylight was rapidly appearing.

4. The attack was carried out with considerable dash notwithstanding the fact that the men had been for 6 weeks employed in trenches under not very favourable conditions.
The attack was gallantly led by Lieut CRABBE who was well supported by Corpl NOURSE and the snipers and by Lieut PAPINEAU & the bomb throwers.

5. Major HAMILTON GAULT and Lieut COLQUHOUN had previously carried out a reconnaissance in the neighbourhood of the German sap, and brought back valuable information regarding the enemys trenches. Lieut COLQUHOUN went out a second time but never returned.

6). Casualties.

Killed. 5 other ranks.

Wounded. Major Gault. Lieut CRABBE and 7 other ranks.

Missing. Lieut COLQUHOUN and 2 others.

Total. 5 Killed. 9 wounded & 2 missing.

13

Appendix XV

16

1580. Feby 28th AAA. I heartily congratulate you and your gallant men on your successful operations this morning AAA Please express to Lieut CRABBE and the party he led my great appreciation of their services × Repeated 2nd Army and 5th Corps

Commander-in-Chief.

14

17 28/2/15

Following message from fifth Corps received begins The Corps Commander has great pleasure in transmitting to you the following message from Second Army Nine Eighteen Am. aaa Begins The Army Commander wishes you to express to the P.P.C.L.I. his appreciation of the grand piece of work performed by them this morning ends

BRIGADE MAJOR.

16

18 28/2/15

GENERAL PLUMER wires please give my heartiest Congratulations to the P.P.C.L.I. on their Gallant and useful Exploit.

BRIGADE Major

17

28/2/15

Well done P.P.C Congratulation on Your Splendid Work

Gen'l Snow. 10.30 A.M.

20

20

28/2/15

Twenty Eighth Division wires hearty Congratulations.

Brigade Major.

19

28/2/15 .. 21

Heartiest Congratulations on Success last Night.

1st Canadian Division. 10.15 Am

80th Infantry Brigade.

27th Division.

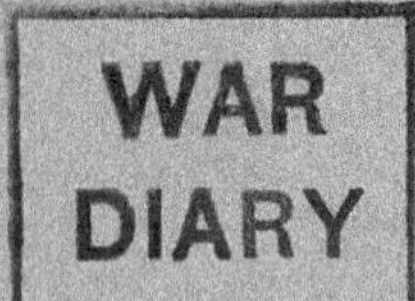

PRINCESS PATRICIA'S CANADIAN LIGHT INFANTRY.

M A R C H

1 9 1 5

Attached:

Appendix XVI.

Instructions regarding War Diaries and Intelligence Summaries are contained in F. S. Regs., Part II. and the Staff Manual respectively. Title pages will be prepared in manuscript.

WAR DIARY
or
INTELLIGENCE SUMMARY.
(Erase heading not required.)

Army Form C. 2118.

Hour, Date, Place	Summary of Events and Information	Remarks and references to Appendices
1. 3. 15.	Enemy bombed trench 21 heavily during the day practically demolishing the parapet. One section of the trench having lost heavily withdrew their place being taken by No 3.	
	Relieved at night by 3rd K.R.R. Major WARD severely wounded. 4th K.R.R. again attacked Sap & converted ~~them~~ it to our own use. Battalion remained at VOORMEZEELE	[illegible]
	till 4 am 2.3.15. Casualties during period 27.2.15 to 1.3.15. Officers. 3 wounded 1 missing. Other ranks 17 killed 44 wounded 2 missing. Total 67.	1.3.15. Draft of 146 NCOs & men [following 8 officers] joined. [Capt S.H. HILL, Capt N.C. OGILVIE, Capt C.H. MOORHEAD, Lieuts C.K. BANNING, A.M. GOW, N.A.E. EDWARDS, J.S. HARVEY 4th L.]
2. 3. 15.	In billets at DICKEBUSH. Working parties by night from all Coys except No 2. at work on new trench 21.	[illegible]
DICKEBUSH 3. 3. 15.	In billets. Working parties on new 21.	
" 4. 3. 15.	In billets. Working parties on new 21. 3 men wounded.	[illegible]
" 5. 3. 15.	No 3. took over trenches 23 A. 23 B. 23 C. from Cheshire Regt 28th Div. 2 men killed 2 wounded.	
" 6. 3. 15.	No 4 relieved No 3 Coy. in trenches 23 A B & C. Enemy's trenches heavily bombarded during the day. Sap & trenches in front of 20. 21 blown to pieces. Sgt CONNOR killed and 3 men wounded.	[illegible]
7. 3. 15.	No 1 Coy relieved No 4 in trenches 23. A. B. C. All quiet.	

2

(73989) W4141—463. 400,000. 9/14. H.&J.Ltd. Forms/C. 2118/10.

Instructions regarding War Diaries and Intelligence Summaries are contained in F. S. Regs., Part II. and the Staff Manual respectively. Title pages will be prepared in manuscript.

WAR DIARY or

INTELLIGENCE SUMMARY.

(Erase heading not required.)

Army Form C. 2118.

Hour, Date, Place		Summary of Events and Information	Remarks and references to Appendices
	8. 3. 15	No 2 Coy relieved No 1 in trenches. 2 saps begun towards German lines from 23 B & 23 C. No 3 Coy at work from 12 m n till 4 am on new 21. Fine night but cold wind. Lieut A M Gow slightly wounded.	HW
	9. 3. 15	No 4 Coy relieved No 2 Coy in trenches.	HW
	10. 3. 15	No 3 Coy relieved No 4 Coy " " No 1 paraded 8 pm and worked till 3.30 am on new trench 21.	HW
7 pm.	11. 3. 15	Battalion less No 3 Coy marched to rest billets at WESTOUTRE. LEINSTER Regt relieved No 3 Coy at midnight. No 3 arrived WESTOUTRE 6 am 12.3.15.	HW
WESTOUTRE	12. 3. 15	Bn in Army Reserve ready to turn out at half hour notice.	HW
"	13. 3. 15	Bn out of Army Reserve ready at 1 hour notice. 7 men rejoined from Hosp ROUEN.	HW
" 4.30 pm	14. 3. 15	Bn warned to be ready to turn out a moments notice.	
5.30 pm.		Bn ordered to fall in.	
7.30 pm	"	Marched to DICKIEBUSH & thence on to ST ELOI where Bn was ordered to assist in counter attack on German trenches west of the MOUND in cooperation with 4th Bn R.B. Lieut CAMERON & 7 NCOs & men killed and Lieut STEWART & LANE and 17 NCOs & men wounded.	HW Report on the action Appendix XVI HW

(73989) W4141—463. 400,000. 9/14. H.&J.Ltd. Forms/C. 2118/10.

Army Form C. 2118.

Instructions regarding War Diaries and Intelligence Summaries are contained in F. S. Regs., Part II. and the Staff Manual respectively. Title pages will be prepared in manuscript.

WAR DIARY
or
INTELLIGENCE SUMMARY.

(Erase heading not required.)

Hour, Date, Place	Summary of Events and Information	Remarks and references to Appendices
4am. 15. 3. 15.	Battalion ordered to return to DICKIEBUSH. Remained in bivouac during the day & moved into huts at night. No 2 Coy remained holding the breastwork.	HM
DICKIEBUSH. 16. 3. 15.	In huts. No 2 Coy returned about midnight.	
" 17. 3. 15.	3 Coys employed at night digging on second line behind St ELOI known as CANADIAN Support trenches.	HM
18. 3. 15.	Bn relieved 3rd K.R.R in trenches 21 22 23 A B & C & in left bit of breastwork	Casualties 17th to 21st: Officers K 2, W 2; O. ranks K 9, W 22; totals 11, 24; 35
19. 3. 15.	Pretty quiet throughout the day. few shells came near SHELLEY F^m. Lieut NIVEN wounded near Canal bridge on the YPRES ROAD. Lieut EARDLEY WILMOT Killed in trench 22. Lieut CAREW MARTIN slightly wounded.	HM
20. 3. 15.	Relieved at night by 3rd Bn K.R.R.C. Lieut Col F.D. FARQUHAR mortally wounded & died at 2 30 am. Bn returned to billets in DICKIEBUSH.	HM
DICKIEBUSH 21. 3. 15.	Lieut Col FARQUHAR buried in the Battalion Cemetery at VOORMEZELE. Revd Percival Comeau Chaplain to 2nd KSLI officiated.	HM
22. 3. 15.	Battalion relieved 3rd Bn K.R.R in trenches as before.	HM

(73989) W4141—463. 400,000. 9/14. H&J.Ltd. Forms/C. 2118/10.

Instructions regarding War Diaries and Intelligence Summaries are contained in F. S. Regs., Part II. and the Staff Manual respectively. Title pages will be prepared in manuscript.

or

INTELLIGENCE SUMMARY.

(*Erase heading not required.*)

Hour, Date, Place		Summary of Events and Information	Remarks and references to Appendices
	23. 3. 15.	Quiet except for few shells near SHELLY F^m + trouble from German trench mortar directed against 22.	
	24. 3. 15.	Line taken over by Battalion of MIDDLESEX Reg^t under Col. STEPHENSON. Relief completed at midnight. B^n marched to billets near POPERINGHE [halting at DICKIEBUSH for tea: into billets about 5 am]	HW.
POPERINGHE	25. 3. 15 to 27. 3. 15	In rest billets at POPERINGHE. Weather fine. Cold wind + frosty nights.	HW.
"	28. 3. 15	Draft of 66 joined B^n including 24 old hands. Lieutenants R.T. CRAWFORD, J.W. VANDENBERG and W.H. BOTHWELL accompanied it.	
	30. 3. 15.	B^n inspected by the Corps Comm^dr Sir H. PLUMER + Div^l Comm^dr Maj Gen SNOW. both of whom spoke in highest terms of the work done by the Batn.	HW.
	31. 3. 15	Brigade inspected by the Army Comm^dr Sir H. SMITH DORRIEN who in course of his remarks warmly congratulated the B^n	HW.
		Casualties to date	

	K	W.	M.	
Officers.	7	9	1	
Other ranks	76	142	3	Total 238
	83	151	4	

5

A P P E N D I X XVI.

Appendix XVI

6

Report on the action near St ELOI on the night of March 14/15.

The Battalion was billeted in WESTOUTRE when orders were received about 5.30 pm on 14th Mar to fall in on Bn Alarm Post. Bn marched about 7 pm at ZEVECOTEN touch was gained with 3rd Bn KRRC behind which unit we marched to DICKEBUSH. About 9.30 pm we proceeded to KRUISTRAATHOEK X roads where a short halt was made and subsequently to VOORMEZELE where the Batt. was drawn up on the road ~~H~~ running N.E towards Cross roads in I 19.d.

Owing to reports from stragglers that the Germans were advancing in large numbers towards the Eastern edge of VOORMEZELE from the S.E. precautions were taken against surprise by the most Easterly Coy of the Bn (No 4).

Soon after 2 am orders were given me personally by the G.O.C. 80th Infantry Brigade to cooperate with 4th Bn R.B. in an attack on the St ELOI "Mound" which had been lost earlier in the day, the zone of operations of the Batt being to the East of the VOORMEZELE – OOSTAVERNE road.

The actual situation in the front line was still obscure. It was known that the Mound & certain trenches to the West of it where in German hands.

To the East, we were known to have lost Trenches 19 & 20. It was uncertain whether 21 was still held or whether the whole of the Breastwork was in our possession

It appeared to me to be preferable to proceed towards SHELLEY'S FARM. If 21 and the left of the breastwork had fallen, they would have been attacked at once;

If not they would cover the commencement of an attack along the German line against 20, 19 + the Mound successively.
The alternative was to advance Southward with the right on the YPRES - ST ELOI Road; this would have meant slow progress through the enclosures round ST ELOI + the subsequent attack would have been exposed to heavy flanking fire from 19 + 20.
The progress of the Battalion was necessarily slow. The street in VOORMEZEELE was full of stragglers, touch was difficult to maintain across country without constant short halts + the alarmist reports from stragglers made it necessary to keep a screen of Scouts in front none of which things made for rapid progress.
I ascertained from Major PROWSE in ST ELOI that trench 20 had been retaken and modified plans accordingly. Instead of going to SHELLEY FARM our objective was changed to the Breastwork 200 yds West of it.
We reached this point about 20 minutes before broad daylight and an attack was organized by 1 Coy (No 2) against Trench 19 via the back of 20. This was made in 3 parties, the first two being composed of 1 platoon + the third of 2 platoons.
This attack failed to make progress against the very heavy machine gun fire from the Mound which completely swept the ground: to reinforce with another Coy appeared to me to be useless sacrifice once the element of surprise had been eliminated. I had already sent back one Coy. and after leaving 3 platoons to hold the right

of the Breastwork next door to the mound, the rest of the Battn was withdrawn to VOORMEZELE and reached DICKEBUSH about 8 am.
Our casualties amounted to 1 officer killed & 2 wounded & 7 NCOs & men killed & 17 wounded. Total 27.
The Battalion behaved with great steadiness throughout the somewhat trying experiences of the night and withdrew over open ground in daylight without leaving a wounded man behind.
It is much to be regretted that owing to being overtaken by daylight, more could not be effected.
All ranks behaved very well but there was no individual sufficiently conspicuous to merit his name being especially put forward for consideration.

I have the honour to be
Sir
Your obedient Servant
Sd. F. D. Farquhar
Lt. Col.
Comdg. P.P.C.L.I.

80th Infantry Brigade.

27th Division.

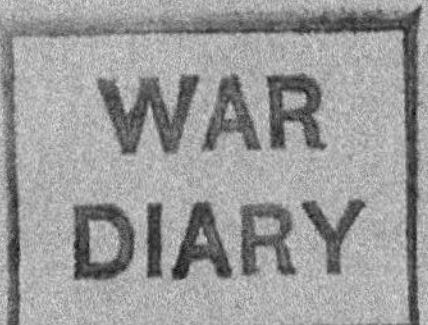

PRINCESS PATRICIA'S CANADIAN LIGHT INFANTRY.

A P R I L

1 9 1 5

WAR DIARY
or
INTELLIGENCE SUMMARY.
(*Erase heading not required.*)

Army Form C. 2118.

1915 Hour, Date, Place		Summary of Events and Information	Remarks and references to Appendices
April 1st to 4th	POPERINGHE	In billets	
April 5th	8.45 am	[Marched via VLAMERTINGHE] to YPRES [and billeted	HM
7th	5.30 pm	No 3 & 4 Coys under Capt HILL occupied dugouts in Close support to the Brigade near the ETANG de BELLEWAARDE. Draft of 37 N.C.Os & men rejoined the Bn	HM
8th		Officers visited trenches to be occupied by their Coys the next night. HM	HM
9th	7.30 pm	Bn marched from YPRES and relieved 4th Bn Rifle Brigade in trenches B.C. & S.S. in POLYGONE DE ZONNEBEKE	HM Sketch & short report Appendix XVII
11th	4 pm	Enemy shelled C trench with H.E. but did no damage.	
	12 m.n.	Relieved by 4th Bn Rifle Brigade. Relief complete at midnight. Casualties [3 men killed and 4 wounded] Draft of 26	
12th		N.C.Os & men rejoined Bn. Weather fine	HM
13th	VLAMERTINGHE	Marched to huts at VLAMERTINGHE and arrived 6 am. 11.30 pm A Zeppelin came over camp & dropped 6 bombs. No damage. Sir H. PLUMER the Corps Commander visited the Battalion.	HM HM
14th		Marched to YPRES and in evening took over trenches from 4th R.B. Nos. 3 & 4 Coys in trenches Nos 1 & 2 Coys in support	
15th		Rumours of expected attack [illegible]	

Instructions regarding War Diaries and Intelligence Summaries are contained in F. S. Regs., Part II. and the Staff Manual respectively. Title pages will be prepared in manuscript.

or INTELLIGENCE SUMMARY.

(Erase heading not required.)

P.P.C.L.I.

1915 Hour, Date, Place	Summary of Events and Information	Remarks and references to Appendices
Apl 17th	Relieved by 4th R.B. and returned to billets in YPRES. Casualties 4 killed 3 wounded.	AWH
" 18th YPRES	Remained in billets in YPRES	AWH
" 19th "	" " " " " Casualties 4 men wounded.	AWH
" 20 "	Heavily shelled in YPRES. Btn. turned out of Barracks in afternoon & waited round pond till time to move off in evening. Moved up to trenches in POLYGONE WOOD and took over from 4th R.B. Nos. 1 & 2 Coys in trenches 3 & 4 Coys in support. Casualties 2 men wounded	[Cas 1st – 21st K 7 W 1 + 21 AWH
" 21st POLYGONE WD	Btn. remained in trenches without relief owing to battle being fought to North in neighbourhood of ST JULIEN. Btn. subjected daily to a certain amount of shelling. [Casualties 3 men wounded & Lt Bothwell wounded.	AWH
" 22nd "	Remained in occupation of trenches in POLYGONE WOOD. [Casualties ~~Lt Bothwell~~ 3 men wounded also 2 others slightly at duty	AWH
" 23 "	Still occupy trenches [Casualties 6 men wounded. Barracks in YPRES shelled & we had casualties 1 man killed 1 man missing believed under debris one man wounded Sergt Cook McSpirity.	AWH
" 24 "	Still occupy same trenches [Casualties 10 men wounded & 3 slightly 1 man killed. Transport & details were moved from YPRES to BUSSEBOOM	AWH
" 25 "	POLYGONE WOOD trenches [Casualties Lt Bainsmith & Capt Ogilvie wounded 6 men wounded]	AWH

(73989) W4141—463. 400,000. 9/14. H.&J.Ltd. Forms/C. 2118/10.

Summaries are contained in F. S. Regs., Part II. and the Staff Manual respectively. Title pages will be prepared in manuscript.

INTELLIGENCE SUMMARY.

(Erase heading not required.)

P.P.C.L.I.

1915 Hour, Date, Place	Summary of Events and Information	Remarks and references to Appendices
Apl 26th POLYGONE WOOD	Still hold same trenches [Casualties 9 men wounded.	HWK
" 27 " "	Occupy same trenches in Wood. Casualties [1 man killed and 10 men wounded	HWK
" 28 " "	Still POLYGONE WOOD trenches [Casualties 5 men wounded & 1 man killed	HWK
" 29 " "	" " " " [Casualties 3 men killed and 1 wounded at duty)	HWK
" 30 " "	[Casualties 6 men wounded Capt Grey slightly wounded.	HWK
~~May 1st~~ " "		
		Ca 22nd–30th K 6 W.3 + 53. M.1

(73989) W4141—463. 400,000. 9/14. H.&J.Ltd. Forms/C. 2118/10.

80th Infantry Brigade.

27th Division.

WAR DIARY

PRINCESS PATRICIA'S CANADIAN LIGHT INFANTRY.

M A Y

(1.5.15 - 1.6.15)

1 9 1 5

or

INTELLIGENCE SUMMARY.

(Erase heading not required.)

Instructions regarding War Diaries and Intelligence Summaries are contained in F. S. Regs., Part II. and the Staff Manual respectively. Title pages will be prepared in manuscript.

P.P.C.L.I.

Hour, Date, Place	Summary of Events and Information	Remarks and references to Appendices
1915 MAY 1st POLYGONE WOOD	10th day in trenches at POLYGONE WOOD. Casualties 9 men wounded	[illegible]
2 " "	11th " " " " " " " none	[illegible]
3	Orders received to withdraw to a subsidiary line. The Batn. to go through the lines & go into rest in G.H.Q. trenches in the night. Further order received that owing to K.S.L.I. having been ordered North Btn would occupy the trenches in Subsidiary line. Casualties during day 2 men killed 3 wounded	
8 P.M.	Two Support Coys under Capt [illegible] withdrew & occupy subsidiary line running N from ETANG BELLEWAARDE to Railway	
9 P.M.	Half trench parties withdrew & occupied support trenches in subsidiary line	
10.30 P.M.	Half remaining trench parties withdrew to support trenches	
12 Midnight	Remaining parties (except 15 men under [illegible] who remained and acted as rear guard to cover the withdrawal) withdrew under Lt. Col. Buller & by 3 A.M. Btn. was in occupation of new line without casualties	[illegible]
May 4th	Men worked hard all night on new trenches but by 7 A.M. the enemy were noticed advancing over crest of ridge to our Right & by 9 A.M. Enemy's Artillery began shelling the trenches & this	[illegible]

2

Instructions regarding War Diaries and Intelligence Summaries are contained in F. S. Regs., Part II. and the Staff Manual respectively. Title pages will be prepared in manuscript.

WAR DIARY
or
INTELLIGENCE SUMMARY.
(Erase heading not required.)

P.P.C.L.I.

Army Form C. 2118.

Hour, Date, Place	Summary of Events and Information	Remarks and references to Appendices
1915 MAY 4th BELLEWAARDE LAKE	heavy shelling continued throughout the day, trenches in many places were blown in. Nos. 1 & 2 Coys in the fire line trench lost heavily. 26 men killed 96 men wounded two of which died two days later.	
	Btn. was relieved by KSLI at 10 p.m. and withdrew to G.H.Q. line near YPRES at junction of Railway & YPRES MENIN ROAD	HWB
" 5th G.H.Q. line	Enemy shelled G.H.Q at intervals during day Lieut Col. H.C. Buller and Lieut A.M. Gow wounded.	
	Major Gault & Lieut Cornish with draft of 47 other ranks joined the Batn the evening of 4th Lt Clark & Lt Newton joined on 5th	HWB
" 6th G.H.Q. line	Remained at G.H.Q. trenches all day were shelled in afternoon casualties 2 killed 9 wounded	
8 45 PM	Btn left for trenches in front of BELLEWAARDE LAKE and relieved KSLI relief complete by 11-30 P.M. Nos 3 & 4 Coy firing line ~~1 & 2~~ support	HWB
" 7th BELLEWAARDE LAKE	Shelling started by Germans about 9 A.M. and considerable damage done to fire trenches casualties 2 men killed 13 wounded (Capt Gray & Lt Cornish were sent back sick in evening. Nos 1 & 2 Coy relieved 3 & 4 Coys in fire trenches.	HWB
" 8th 4 A.M.	Shelling by Germans started chiefly from our right flank which enfiladed our fire trenches this guns were [illegible] by 5.30 [illegible] about this time some Germans were noticed coming down hill directly in front of us and we opened rapid fire on them	

3

Instructions regarding War Diaries and Intelligence Summaries are contained in F. S. Regs., Part II. and the Staff Manual respectively. Title pages will be prepared in manuscript.

Army Form C. 2118.

WAR DIARY
or
INTELLIGENCE SUMMARY.
(Erase heading not required.)

P.P.C.L.I.

4

1915 Hour, Date, Place	Summary of Events and Information (Cont'd.)	Remarks and references to Appendices
MAY 8 6 A.M.	All our telephone wires were cut by this time both to Brigade & back to trenches so all Signallers, Pioneers, Orderlies & Servants were ordered into Support trenches and shortly afterwards the advance by Germans was checked and any not sheltered by buildings or dead crawled back over crest of ridge to trenches. Germans had two [or] possibly three Machine guns in buildings & were sweeping our parapet both in Fire and Support trenches. An orderly went back to Brigade [illegible] notifying them [illegible]	
7 A.M.	Major Gault was severely hit (by shell in left arm & left thigh) shelling by heavy Howitzers using all high explosive & field guns started again in heavy bombardment both in Fire & Support trenches. Fire trench on right being blown in at several points. [illegible] by orderly to Brigade notifying them we were being heavily shelled & asking for reinforcements as our casualties were heavy.	
9 A.M.	Cessation in shelling and Germans again attempted to advance but heavy fire from our Machine Guns & rifles checked them & forced them to retire & take cover at this time P.P.C.L.I. accounted for many of the enemy. Lieut Martin & [illegible] were hit coming out of communicating trench with [illegible] wounded. Capt Hill & Lt [illegible] hit also.	[initials]

(73989) W4141—463. 400,000. 9/14. H.&J.Ltd. Forms/C. 2118/10.

Instructions regarding War Diaries and Intelligence Summaries are contained in F. S. Regs., Part II. and the Staff Manual respectively. Title pages will be prepared in manuscript.

WAR DIARY
or
INTELLIGENCE SUMMARY.
(Erase heading not required.)

1915 Hour, Date, Place	Summary of Events and Information	Remarks and references to Appendices
MAY 8th 9.30 AM	[illegible]	
10.25 AM	[illegible]	

(73989) W4141—463. 400,000. 9/14. H.&J.Ltd. Forms/C. 2118/10.

Instructions regarding War Diaries and Intelligence Summaries are contained in F. S. Regs., Part II. and the Staff Manual respectively. Title pages will be prepared in manuscript.

or

INTELLIGENCE SUMMARY.

(*Erase heading not required.*)

Hour, Date, Place	Summary of Events and Information	Remarks and references to Appendices
1915	Cont'd	
May 8th 12 A.M.	Snipers had been detected, when taking messages to Brigade & reserve Batn kept in rear of BELLEWAARDE LAKE during the morning as ground the road was continually shelled. A message was sent asking Brigade for more S.A.A. as rifle fire was brisk at all times.	
1-30 P.M.	Our Reserve 4 R.B. was sent in as reinforcements to support & which gave them a cheer as they came up & placed them in our reserve [illegible] in two orders watch our flank as we were unable from trench work at [illegible] ground. They were in line with our support trench behind the ridge. They are [illegible] a machine gun and section that did good service	
2 P.M.	I went with orderly to BELLEWAARDE LAKE dugouts as ordered by Brigade to telephone G.O.C. 80th Infty Bde. complete details of situation returning at 2-20 P.M. orderlies accompanying me both going and coming were hit by High Explosive Shells.	
3 P.M.	A platoon of K.S.L.I. under an Officer reached our support line with 20 boxes S.A.A. which was distributed. This party also acted as reinforcement & occupied left end of support line. H.W.	

(73989) W4141—463. 400,000. 9/14. H.&J.Ltd. Forms/C. 2118/10.

Instructions regarding War Diaries and Intelligence Summaries are contained in F. S. Regs., Part II. and the Staff Manual respectively. Title pages will be prepared in manuscript.

or

INTELLIGENCE SUMMARY.

(Erase heading not required.)

P.P.C.L.I.

1915 Hour, Date, Place	Summary of Events and Information (Contd)	Remarks and references to Appendices
MAY 8th 4 P.M.	Made tour of support trenches & found we were out of touch with Regt. on our left a gap of fifty yards was unoccupied. I placed [illegible] in the gap & inform [illegible] of happenings there. Shortly afterwards I was informed that Monmouth Regt on left of K.O.Y.L.I. had withdrawn to trenches 300 yards in rear and about 5.30 was informed that K.O.Y.L.I. had also withdrawn to same line of trenches. Another attempt by Germans to advance was stopped by our rifle fire although some reached our trench on right that could not be [illegible] from [illegible] trench but I believe at this was that [illegible] men alive at the point.	
11.30 P.M.	We were relieved by 3rd K.R.R. who gave us permission to bury our dead that were in support & communication trenches as it was impossible inexpedient to attempt to reach the fire trenches. Our casualties were as follows killed Lieut. Edwards died of wounds Lieut. Crawford, missing Lieut. Denison, Lieut. Lane. wounded Major Gault, Capt. Adamson, Capt. Hill, Lieut. De Bay [illegible]	

(73989) W4141—463. 400,000. 9/14. H.&J.Ltd. Forms/C. 2118/10.

Instructions regarding War Diaries and Intelligence Summaries are contained in F.S. Regs., Part II. and the Staff Manual respectively. Title pages will be prepared in manuscript.

WAR DIARY
or
INTELLIGENCE SUMMARY.

(*Erase heading not required.*)

P.P.C.L.I.

1915 Hour, Date, Place	(Contd) Summary of Events and Information	Remarks and references to Appendices
MAY 8	[illegible] Other ranks 93 killed [illegible] 203 wounded.	[illegible]
MAY 9th	[illegible] H.Q. [illegible] Railway [illegible] at 2-30 AM [illegible] to proceed to LILLE GATE YPRES and [illegible] [illegible] wounded.	[illegible]
10th	YPRES [illegible] DICKEBUSCH [illegible] ZILLEBEKE LAKE [illegible] 2 wounded [illegible] digging party [illegible]	[illegible]
11th	[illegible]	[illegible]
12th	YPRES [illegible] and marched [illegible] about 7 AM. Casualties [illegible] wounded [illegible] YPRES [illegible]	[illegible]
13	[illegible] [illegible] HOOGE CHATEAU [illegible] 4th R.B. in trenches [illegible]	[illegible]

8

Instructions regarding War Diaries and Intelligence Summaries are contained in F. S. Regs., Part II. and the Staff Manual respectively. Title pages will be prepared in manuscript.

or

INTELLIGENCE SUMMARY.

(Erase heading not required.)

P.P.C.L.I.

1915 Hour, Date, Place	Summary of Events and Information	Remarks and references to Appendices
14th May	In trenches at HOOGE CHATEAU. All quiet.	F
15th "	Still in trenches at HOOGE CHATEAU. Major Pelly rejoined from sick leave & took command from Lieut & Adj Niven.	F
16th May	All quiet in trenches [a few "whiz bangs" sent over Btn Head Quarters]	F
17th May	All quiet. Relieved by Queens Bays and 11th Hussars at 10 pm – returned to bivouac at BUSSEBOOM	F
18th May	In bivouac at BUSSEBOOM	F
19th May	80th Brigade inspected by the C in C, Sir John French who spoke in highest possible terms of the P.P.C.L.I and also referred to the loss the Regiment sustained when Colonel Farquhar was killed.	F

(73989) W4141—463. 400,000. 9/14. H.&J.Ltd. Forms/C. 2118/10.

WAR DIARY
or
INTELLIGENCE SUMMARY.
(Erase heading not required.)

Instructions regarding War Diaries and Intelligence Summaries are contained in F. S. Regs., Part II. and the Staff Manual respectively. Title pages will be prepared in manuscript.

P.P.C.L.I.

1915 Hour, Date, Place	Summary of Events and Information	Remarks and references to Appendices
20th May	In bivouac at BUSSEBOOM	P
21st May	Still at BUSSEBOOM. The men had hot baths at POPERINGHE.	
	The following new officers arrived, having been sent as a reinforcement from the 11th Canadian Bn. Shorncliffe.	
	2 Major Wayne, Major Lindsay, 5 Capt Arnold, Capt Pearson, Capt Cooper, Capt Mauner, 12 Lieut Reid, Lieut Settlers, Lieut Newton, Lieut Smith, Lieut Sparks, Lieut de Bateland, Lieut McDermid, Lieut Ferguson, Lieut Strath, Capt Forbes, Lieut Fraser, Lieut Stewart, Lieut Ralph	
	Lieut Stanley-Jones also rejoined from England	P
22nd & 23rd May	In bivouac at BUSSEBOOM	P

(73989) W4141—463. 400,000. 9/14. H.&J.Ltd. Forms/C. 2118/10.

or
INTELLIGENCE SUMMARY.
(*Erase heading not required.*)

P.P.C.L.I.

1915 Hour, Date, Place	Summary of Events and Information	Remarks and references to Appendices
24th May	Very heavy bombardment heard at dawn in direction of YPRES.	
5.30 a.m.	Received to turn out in half an hour	
6 a.m.	Brigade marched to a point on the POPERINGHE – VLAMERTINGHE Road, the P.P.C.L.I. in rear, where we waited for 6 hours.	
noon	Received orders to proceed to the LILLE GATE, YPRES going via the South of the town. From there the 2nd K.S.L.I. + 4th K.R.R.C. moved on to the level crossing on the YPRES – MENIN road to form the firing line in a counter attack on the trenches at HOOGE CHATEAU which had been lost in a gas attack.	
	A brigade of the 27th Division counter attacked on the left of the K.S.L.I. while on the right the 4th K.R.R.C. endeavoured unsuccessfully to get in touch with the cavalry in ZOUAVE WOOD.	
	The 3rd K.R.R.C. + 4th R.B. formed a supporting	

(73989) W4141—463. 400,000. 9/14. H.&J.Ltd. Forms/C. 2118/10.

WAR DIARY
or
INTELLIGENCE SUMMARY.
(*Erase heading not required.*)

Instructions regarding War Diaries and Intelligence Summaries are contained in F.S. Regs., Part II. and the Staff Manual respectively. Title pages will be prepared in manuscript.

P.P.C.L.I.

12

Hour, Date, Place	Summary of Events and Information	Remarks and references to Appendices
1915	line while] the P.P.C.L.I. moved to the G.H.Q. line near the MENIN Road level crossing & obtained tools & sandbags ready to assist in digging the firing line in when the attack was complete.	
8.30 pm		
25th May 2.15 am	Day broke when the attack (which was unsuccessful) was held up about 1000 yards East of the Railway crossing.	
	The P.P.C.L.I. then took the tools up under a somewhat heavy shell fire & rifle fire & on completion of this duty the Battalion was ordered to occupy the trench near the LILLE GATE.	
	Casualties 1 Officer (Major Lindsay) + [illegible] men wounded	
4 am	Reached the LILLE GATE & remained all day being periodically shelled.	
8.15 pm	Proceeded to level crossing in MENIN Road.	

Instructions regarding War Diaries and Intelligence Summaries are contained in F. S. Regs., Part II. and the Staff Manual respectively. Title pages will be prepared in manuscript.

INTELLIGENCE SUMMARY.

(*Erase heading not required.*)

P.P.C.L.I.

Hour, Date, Place	Summary of Events and Information	Remarks and references to Appendices
1915	where we met transport with Rations, tools & sandbags.	
	Moved up the road 1 mile to the East & dug a new line of trenches to fill a gap between the MENIN Road & ZOUAVE Wood.	
2 a.m.	Trenches completed at dawn, Battn returned to LILLE GATE.	
	Sent two officers Capt Penleigh (?) & Lieut Sparks to 2 K.S.L.I. who had lost all their officers except two.	
	Casualties while digging trenches – 2 men wounded	
26th May 1915	Remained at LILLE GATE – was shelled – little or no casualties –	
	1 officer (Lieut Stanley-Jones (?)) & [illegible] men wounded	
12 midnight	Received orders to return to bivouac (?) at BUSSEBOOM	
2 a.m.	Reached BUSSEBOOM.	
	Received report from 2 K.S.L.I. that Lieut Sparks was wounded	13

(73989) W4141—463. 400,000. 9/14. H.&J.Ltd. Forms/C. 2118/10.

Instructions regarding War Diaries and Intelligence Summaries are contained in F. S. Regs., Part II. and the Staff Manual respectively. Title pages will be prepared in manuscript.

WAR DIARY or INTELLIGENCE SUMMARY.

(*Erase heading not required.*)

Hour, Date, Place	Summary of Events and Information	Remarks and references to Appendices
27th May 1915	In bivouac at BUSSE BOOM	
28th May	The Brigadier (Gen Smith) inspected the transport in the morning	
6 pm	General Sir Allenby commanding the 5th Corps paid us a farewell visit	
29th May 30th "	In bivouac at BUSSE BOOM " " "	
31st May 4 am	Marched to DRANOUTRE near LOCRE & went into huts.	
1st June 1915 4.30 am	Marched to STEENWERKE & billeted in 3 farms	
3 pm	Officers went by motor bus to ARMENTIERES & visited the trenches we are to occupy	P

80th Infantry Brigade.

27th Division.

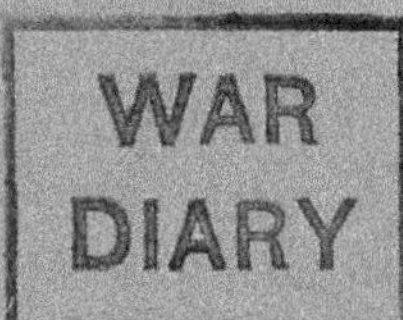

PRINCESS PATRICIA'S CANADIAN LIGHT INFANTRY.

J U L Y

1 9 1 5

Instructions regarding War Diaries and Intelligence Summaries are contained in F. S. Regs., Part II. and the Staff Manual respectively. Title pages will be prepared in manuscript.

WAR DIARY
or
INTELLIGENCE SUMMARY.
(Erase heading not required.)

Army Form C. 2118.

Hour, Date, Place	Summary of Events and Information	Remarks and references to Appendices
1915 July 1st	The Battalion went into trenches at L'EPINETTE. No. 4, No. 3, No. 2 Coys. went into Fire trenches 77 & part of 78. No Casualties.	[illegible]
2nd	All quiet, good weather.	[illegible]
3rd	All quiet, no casualties.	[illegible]
4th	All quiet one man wounded.	[illegible]
5th	H.Q. & two companies came out to billets in ARMENTIERES and two Companies remained in support. All quiet no casualties.	[illegible]
" 6th	Shell burst in Transport billet in town killing one man and wounding three others. Two Companies in billets relieved the two Companies in support.	[illegible]
" 7th	All quiet no casualties.	[illegible]
" 8th	All quiet no casualties.	[illegible]
" 9th	Regiment went into trenches again 78 & 79 at L'EPINETTE, one Company in support no casualties.	[illegible]
" 10th	All quiet one man wounded.	[illegible]
" 11th	" " no casualties.	[illegible]
" 12th	" " " "	[illegible]
" 13th	" " " "	[illegible]

2

(73989) W4141—463. 400,000. 9/14. H.&J.Ltd. Forms/C. 2118/10.

Instructions regarding War Diaries and Intelligence Summaries are contained in F. S. Regs., Part II. and the Staff Manual respectively. Title pages will be prepared in manuscript.

WAR DIARY or INTELLIGENCE SUMMARY.

(*Erase heading not required.*)

1915 Hour, Date, Place	Summary of Events and Information	Remarks and references to Appendices
July 14th	All quiet no casualties	[illegible]
15th	" "	[illegible]
16th	Relieved in trenches by 4th Northumberland Fusiliers and marched to bivouac at Trois Arbres near Steenwerck very wet night.	[illegible]
17	Remained in camp & rest.	[illegible]
18	" "	[illegible]
19	" "	[illegible]
20	marched to new camp at Petit Moulin farm	[illegible]
21	were inspected by Sir Robert Borden and Prince Arthur of Connaught.	[illegible]
22	Remained in camp & built shelter huts.	[illegible]
23	" " received call from Sir Douglas Haig Commander of 1st Army wet day.	[illegible]
24	In camp wet.	[illegible]
25th	In Camp Fine	[illegible]
26th	In Camp Fine	[illegible]
27th	In camp Fine	[illegible]

Instructions regarding War Diaries and Intelligence Summaries are contained in F. S. Regs., Part II. and the Staff Manual respectively. Title pages will be prepared in manuscript.

WAR DIARY
or
INTELLIGENCE SUMMARY.
(Erase heading not required.) P.P.C.L.I.

Army Form C. 2118.

Hour, Date, Place	Summary of Events and Information	Remarks and references to Appendices
1915 July 28th	Camped at PETIT MOULIN Farm. New draft (McGill) of 244 men and 5 Officers arrived. Officers C. J. T. Stewart, Lieut E.D.C. MARTIN, Lieut S.F.A. MARTIN, Capt. BARCLAY Capt McDOUGAL	[illegible]
29th	The following Officers rejoined from Base Capt GREY Lieut CRABBE and the following Officers joined from Depot Lieut POPE Lieut IRWIN Lieut BEVINGTON.	[illegible]
30th	In Camp	[illegible]
31st	New draft and Officers inspected by Brig Gen Smith	[illegible]

(73989) W4141—463. 400,000. 9/14. H.&J.Ltd. Forms/C. 2118/10.

80th Infantry Brigade.

27th Division.

WAR DIARY

PRINCESS PATRICIA'S CANADIAN LIGHT INFANTRY.

A U G U S T

1 9 1 5

Instructions regarding War Diaries and Intelligence Summaries are contained in F. S. Regs., Part II. and the Staff Manual respectively. Title pages will be prepared in manuscript.

WAR DIARY

or

INTELLIGENCE SUMMARY.

(Erase heading not required.)

Army Form C. 2118.

1915 Hour, Date, Place	Summary of Events and Information	Remarks and references to Appendices
August 1st	Lieut Col Pilly & Officers made a tour of inspection over new line of trenches to be taken over next day. Officers of the Regiment were inspected by new G.O.C. of the 27th Division Major General MILNE	[illegible]
" 2nd	At 9.30 P.M. Nos. 3 and 4 Companies took over fire & support trench #63 from 9th ROYAL SCOTS at RUE du BOIS. Nos. 1 and 2 Companies occupied billets on outskirts of ARMENTIERES. no casualties	[illegible]
" 3rd	All quiet in trenches no casualties	[illegible]
" 4th	All quiet in trenches. Lieut E.D.C. MARTIN was wounded by Machine Gun fire at Dumping Ground and one man killed on fatigue at LA CHAPELLE d'ARMENTIERES.	[illegible]
" 5th	Capt GREY made a reconnaissance in front of trenches and found all clear of enemy patrols. [illegible]	[illegible]
" 6th	In trenches, all quiet, searchlight used by enemy frequently during the night, Orchard at H.Q. shelled but no casualties. Relieved by reserve companies	[illegible]
" 7th	One man slightly wounded, Found dead German in front of lines.	

2

Instructions regarding War Diaries and Intelligence Summaries are contained in F. S. Regs., Part II. and the Staff Manual respectively. Title pages will be prepared in manuscript.

or

INTELLIGENCE SUMMARY.

(*Erase heading not required.*) P. P. C. L. I.

1915 Hour, Date, Place	Summary of Events and Information	Remarks and references to Appendices
August 8th	Reserve Companies #3 & 4 under Col Pelly inspected by Gen. Sam Hughes who spoke about large pensions and	HWN
" 9th	All quiet, work continues building Shell Shelters & wire entanglements	HWN
" 10th	Reserve Companies relieve those in Firing Trench, All quiet	HWN
" 11th	Exceptionally quiet in trenches, no casualties, many fatigue parties	HWN
" 12th	All quiet, Colors Flying at H.Q. to celebrate first birthday of Regiment, receive many congratulations	HWN
" 13th	All quiet	HWN
" 14th	Snipers locate Germans digging sap towards our trench, All quiet, no casualties. Lieut. Lowther of the Westmorland & Cumberland Yeomanry is attached to this Regiment for instruction	HWN
" 15th	All quiet, one man wounded, rain	HWN
" 16th	All quiet, wet day	HWN
" 17	All quiet, one man wounded.	HWN
" 18	All quiet, one man wounded.	HWN

3

Instructions regarding War Diaries and Intelligence Summaries are contained in F. S. Regs., Part II. and the Staff Manual respectively. Title pages will be prepared in manuscript.

INTELLIGENCE SUMMARY.

(*Erase heading not required.*)

PPCLI

1915 Hour, Date, Place	Summary of Events and Information	Remarks and references to Appendices
August 19th	All quiet, constructing Shell Shelters in fire trench no casualties	[illegible]
20th	All quiet, no casualties Four Colonels visit our trenches K	[illegible]
21st	All quiet "	[illegible]
22nd	All quiet "	[illegible]
23rd	All quiet "	[illegible]
24th	All quiet " " A squadron of the Surrey Yeomanry were attached to us in the trenches for instruction They are commanded by Major [illegible] Daw[illegible] night	[illegible]
25th	All quiet, Parties work in front of our fire trench every day digging borrow pit and strengthening parapet	[illegible]
26th	All quiet, [illegible] day.	[illegible]
27th	All quiet Westmorland & Cumberland Yeomanry Machine Gun section under Lieut [illegible] [illegible] to their [illegible].	[illegible]
28th	All quiet, no casualties	[illegible]
29th	All quiet, " " [illegible] day	[illegible]
30th	All quiet We are relieved by [illegible] Regiment and go to rest camp at PETIT MOULIN FARM	[illegible]

Instructions regarding War Diaries and Intelligence Summaries are contained in F. S. Regs., Part II. and the Staff Manual respectively. Title pages will be prepared in manuscript.

or

INTELLIGENCE SUMMARY.

(Erase heading not required.)

PPCLI 3

Hour, Date, Place	Summary of Events and Information	Remarks and references to Appendices
1915 August 31st	In Rest Camp at PETIT MOULIN FARM	

(73989) W4141—463. 400,000. 9/14. H.&J.Ltd. Forms/C. 2118/10.

War Diary

Month of August 1915

Errata

Entry under date	
Aug. 5th	For Grey read, Gray.
Aug. 24th	For Major Colwell read, Major A. Calvert D.S.O.

Addendum

Under date	
Aug. 5th	Add to last line of entry the following; Lieut. Newcombe joins Regiment.

R. T. Pelly Lieut Col
Comdg P.P.C.L.I.

80th Infantry Brigade.

27th Division.

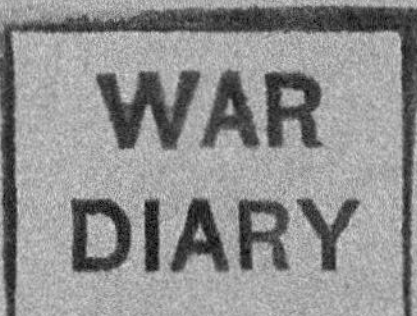

PRINCESS PATRICIA'S CANADIAN LIGHT INFANTRY.

S E P T E M B E R

1 9 1 5

Instructions regarding War Diaries and Intelligence Summaries are contained in F. S. Regs., Part II. and the Staff Manual respectively. Title pages will be prepared in manuscript.

or

INTELLIGENCE SUMMARY.

(*Erase heading not required.*)

P.P.C.L.I.

Hour, Date, Place		Summary of Events and Information	Remarks and references to Appendices
1915 September	1st	Rest Camp at Petit Moulin Farm. Receive large reinforcement of 244 other ranks, 28 old men returned 216 new draft composed of University men chiefly, weather damp. Battalion Strength today 994 the largest since January.	HWN [?]
Rest Camp. Petit Moulin Farm.	2nd	Inspection of new draft and posting them to their Companies.	HWN [?]
	3rd	Furnish working parties of 500 [?] men but heavy rain prevents work being carried out.	HWN [?]
	4th	Wet day. Lieut Nash [?] joins the Battalion & is posted to No 3 Coy.	HWN [?]
	5th	Had Church parades in the morning and played a rugby match in the afternoon with the R. Bs.	E.A.M.
	6th	Drafts inspected this morning by Brig. General ~~Moore~~ Smith. Afterwards nos 1 and 2 companies were inspected in the attack. The regiment supplied a working party of 600 men at Rue du Bois in the evening.	E.A.M.
	7th	Had our sports today. weather very fine and hot. Lieut. Papineau went to England on leave	E.A.M.
	8th	Had our boxing and wrestling bouts today. A/Captain Niven and A/Captain Earl went to England on leave.	E.A.M.

(73989) W4141—463. 400,000. 9/14. H.&J.Ltd. Forms/C. 2118/10.

Instructions regarding War Diaries and Intelligence Summaries are contained in F. S. Regs., Part II. and the Staff Manual respectively. Title pages will be prepared in manuscript.

WAR DIARY
or
INTELLIGENCE SUMMARY.
(Erase heading not required.)

Army Form C. 2118.

P.P.C.L.I.

Hour, Date, Place	Summary of Events and Information	Remarks and references to Appendices
1915 September 9th Petit Moulin Farm.	Weather very hot. Still in rest camp at Petit Moulin Farm.	E.A.M.
10th	Weather still very hot. Lt Cowley reported back to the regiment. The regiment did very well at the brigade horse show and carried off four events and was second in three others.	E.A.M.
11th	Weather still very hot. Still in rest camp at Petit Moulin Farm. Had our concert and prize giving for the sports this evening. Lt Crabbe left for England.	E.A.M.
12th	Weather very warm. Regiment had church parade in the morning, and supplied a small working party in the afternoon.	E.A.M.
13th	Companies went for route marches today but otherwise no activities, weather warm	E.A.M.
14th	The day was quiet and no parades were held until 6.15 in the evening when the regiment moved with the brigade on its way to a new area and were billeted at Pradelles, a village about 3 miles from Hazebrouck.	E.A.M.

(73989) W4141—463. 400,000. 9/14. H.&J.Ltd. Forms/C. 2118/10.

Instructions regarding War Diaries and Intelligence Summaries are contained in F. S. Regs., Part II. and the Staff Manual respectively. Title pages will be prepared in manuscript.

INTELLIGENCE SUMMARY.

(Erase heading not required.)

Hour, Date, Place	Summary of Events and Information	Remarks and references to Appendices
Pradelles Sept. 15th	Today was spent resting in billets and there is nothing of interest to record.	E.A.M.
Sept. 16th	Company route marches were made by all the companies Today. The weather still fine & warm	E.A.M.
Sept. 17th	Today the regiment paraded with the rest of the brigade to take leave of our Corps Commander, General Pulteney. The whole parade was of an exceptionally high order of merit and in saying good bye, General Pulteney reminded the brigade that it was a regular one of the highest repute going to stiffen the front held by one of the new service armies sent across from England quite lately to take over part of the line hitherto held by our allies south of Arras in a most	

(73989) W4141—463. 400,000. 9/14. H.&J.Ltd. Forms/C. 2118/10.

Summaries are contained in F. S. Regs., Part II. and the Staff Manual respectively. Title pages will be prepared in manuscript.

INTELLIGENCE SUMMARY.

(*Erase heading not required.*)

Hour, Date, Place	Summary of Events and Information	Remarks and references to Appendices
	important part of the line. He said further that he considered us very worthy of the duty before us and hoped that the day would come when we would return to his command. In the meantime he wished us all godspeed and the very best of good fortune.	E.A.N.
	The brigade before marching off to battalion parades gave him three cheers.	
Sept 18th	Today the regiment marched into Hazebrouck and entrained at 6 o'clock in the afternoon for our new area in the neighbourhood of Amiens, which we expect to reach at an early hour tomorrow morning.	E.A.N.

Instructions regarding War Diaries and Intelligence Summaries are contained in F. S. Regs., Part II. and the Staff Manual respectively. Title pages will be prepared in manuscript.

or

INTELLIGENCE SUMMARY.

(Erase heading not required.)

P. P. C. L. I.

1915 Hour, Date, Place	Summary of Events and Information	Remarks and references to Appendices
Mericourt Sept. 19th	Arrived at Gillaucourt about 6.30 this morning, after a very satisfactory journey as regards Transport arrangements. The unloading was completed without accident in 40 minutes from time of arrival. The regiment then marched about 6 miles to Mericourt where we bivouacked ~~&~~ in a field just beyond the village. The march discipline was very good and there was no straggling. We were joined about 6 p.m by 2 officers and 25 men of the 82nd Trench Howitzer Battery (Lt. Beard & Lt. Wilmot i/c) They are attached to the 80th Brigade and to the P.P.C.L.I. for quarters and rations.	

(73989) W4141—463. 400,000. 9/14. H.&J.Ltd. Forms C. 2118/10.

Instructions regarding War Diaries and Intelligence Summaries are contained in F. S. Regs., Part II. and the Staff Manual respectively. Title pages will be prepared in manuscript.

INTELLIGENCE SUMMARY.

(*Erase heading not required.*)

P. P. C. L. I.

1915. Hour, Date, Place	Summary of Events and Information	Remarks and references to Appendices
Froissy 20.9.15.	Arrived here at 4.15 p.m. today after a march of 2 hours from Pradelles. The Regiment is quartered in a line of huts along the right bank of the Somme canal. Weather - fine and warm.	E.A.M.
21.9.15.	The regiment remained in quarters all day. Colonel Pelly, Major Gray and one officer per company visited our new Trenches. Weather fine and warm.	E.A.M.
22.9.15.	Remained in quarters all day. A party of officers visited our new Trenches. Weather fine & warm	E.A.M.
23.9.15	Companies practised in attack this morning. Furnished working party of 200 men tonight. Weather becoming stormy with thunder.	E.A.M.

(73989) W4141—463. 400,000. 9/14. H.&J.Ltd. Forms/C. 2118/10.

Summaries are contained in F. S. Regs., Part II. and the Staff Manual respectively. Title pages will be prepared in manuscript.

INTELLIGENCE SUMMARY.

(*Erase heading not required.*)

P.P.C.L.I.

1915. Hour, Date, Place	Summary of Events and Information	Remarks and references to Appendices
24.9.15.	Regiment remained in quarters all day. Companies worked out in extended order. Weather fine and warm. Working party of 200 men in evening.	E.A.M.
25.9.15.	Moved to Cappy this afternoon. No 1 Company and half of No 2 Company (under Lt. Pope and Lt. Irwin) went into Trenches and No 4 company went into support at Eclusiers. Weather was rainy and marching quite sticky.	E.A.M.
26.9.15.	Nothing of interest to record today. Sent a working party of 40 men to dig new fire trenches in the evening. Weather was fair.	E.A.M.
27.9.15.	This evening the remainder of the battalion (no 3 company and no 2 less 2 platoons) marched up to Eclusiers to go into	

(73989) W4141—463. 400,000. 9/14. H.&J.Ltd. Forms/C. 2118/10.

Summaries are contained in F. S. Regs., Part II. and the Staff Manual respectively. Title pages will be prepared in manuscript.

INTELLIGENCE SUMMARY.

(Erase heading not required.)

P. P. C. L. I.

1915 Hour, Date, Place	Summary of Events and Information	Remarks and references to Appendices
27.9.15	Brigade support. One platoon from No 3 Company (LT. NEWCOMBE) and one from No 4 Company (LT COWLEY) went into support with the 4th RIFLE BRIGADE at REDOUTE DES GOBELINES. Weather ~~wet~~ cold and rainy.	E.T.H.
28.9.15	Nothing of importance today. Weather cold and rainy.	E.T.H.
29.9.15.	Nothing of importance Today. weather cold and fine.	
30.9.15	Two platoons which were in support to the ~~Rifle Brigade~~ 4th RIFLE BRIGADE were relieved today by the RIFLE BRIGADE and returned to ECLUSIERS. Weather. Cold & fine.	E.T.H.

9

(73989) W4141—463. 400,000. 9/14. H.&J.Ltd. Forms/C. 2118/10.

80th Infantry Brigade.

27th Division.

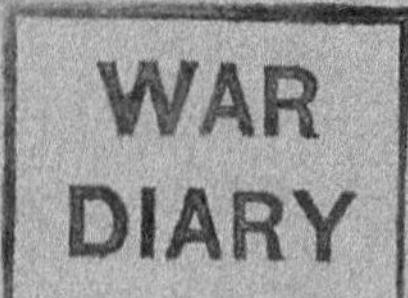

PRINCESS PATRICIA'S CANADIAN LIGHT INFANTRY.

O C T O B E R

1 9 1 5

Army Form C. 2118.

Instructions regarding War Diaries and Intelligence Summaries are contained in F. S. Regs., Part II. and the Staff Manual respectively. Title pages will be prepared in manuscript.

WAR DIARY
or
INTELLIGENCE SUMMARY.
(Erase heading not required.)

P. P. C. L. I.

Hour, Date, Place	Summary of Events and Information	Remarks and references to Appendices
1915 1. 10. 15. In trenches at ~~Frise~~ FRISE.	Today was quiet in the trenches and tonight no 3 company moved up to the fire trenches taking over the line on the left of the canal. no 2 company moved to the trenches immediately on the right of the canal. Weather cold and fine.	E.M.
2. 10. 15.	Today nothing of interest was done. The men were busy improving the trenches in different ways and making new dugouts. Weather fine.	E.M.
3. 10. 15.	Today the enemy have been very active on the right of our trenches. There was quite a lot of sniping and a number of whizz bangs were fired into the trench occupied by no 4	

(73989) W4141—463. 400,000. 9/14. H.&J.Ltd. Forms/C. 2118/10.

Instructions regarding War Diaries and Intelligence Summaries are contained in F. S. Regs., Part II. and the Staff Manual respectively. Title pages will be prepared in manuscript.

INTELLIGENCE SUMMARY.

(Erase heading not required.)

P.P.C.L.I.

Place	Date	Hour	Summary of Events and Information	Remarks and references to Appendices
1915	3.10.15.		company. LT. DE BALLINHARD and LT COWLEY were wounded. Otherwise no casualties. weather very fine.	E.A.M.
	4.10.15.		a very quiet day, a detachment of the BLACK WATCH have come into the Trenches for instruction by LT VAN DEN BERG in machine gun work and a new detachment take their place tomorrow. weather fine	E.A.M.
	5.10.15		Another very quiet day. Two men slightly wounded in the CROWS NEST by a stray bullet. (No A11098) (one from BLACK WATCH) weather wet.	E.A.M.
	6.10.15.		very little activity today and the line begins to show the results of the work done on it particularly the left half which is now in very good condition. Weather damp and unpleasant.	E.A.M.
	7.10.15		Today has been very quiet all along the line and there has been unusually little firing. LT PAPINEAU reported back for duty	

T2134. Wt. W708—776. 500000. 4/15. Sir J. C. & S.

Instructions regarding War Diaries and Intelligence Summaries are contained in F. S. Regs., Part II. and the Staff Manual respectively. Title pages will be prepared in manuscript.

or

INTELLIGENCE SUMMARY.

(Erase heading not required.)

P. P. C. L. I.

Place	Date	Hour	Summary of Events and Information	Remarks and references to Appendices
	7.10.15		A patrol of 8 snipers & 2 grenadiers under Sgt CHRISTIE went out late this afternoon from our left Trench and made their way, crawling through the grass to the German side of the marsh, with a view to intercepting a German patrol believed to pass down the road from LA GRENOUILLÈRE to CURLU about 7 p.m. each evening. Our patrol got safely to the German side of the marsh, and concealed themselves 20 yards from the road. Just after dusk a strong German Patrol came down the road, (consisting of 30 men under an officer) marching in fours and with a flanking party in the marsh. Sgt. CHRISTIE seeing himself hopelessly outnumbered and in danger of being cut off between the two parties resorted to bluff and ordered the Germans to "Hands up". The enemy not complying, our men opened rapid fire, the grenadiers at the same time throwing	E.M.

4

2353 Wt. W2544/1454 700,000 5/15 D. D. & L. A.D.S.S./Forms/C. 2118.

Summaries are contained in F. S. Regs., Part II. and the Staff Manual respectively. Title pages will be prepared in manuscript.

INTELLIGENCE SUMMARY. P.P.C.L.I.

(Erase heading not required.)

Place	Date	Hour	Summary of Events and Information	Remarks and references to Appendices
	7.10.15.		their bombs into the midst of the close mass of men in the road. The Germans threw themselves down and returned the fire of our men while the flanking party closed up. Our two right hand men faced around to meet them and one of our men killed a German who had come within a couple of yards of him. The enemy after throwing 2 or 3 bombs which did no damage began to crawl away leaving several dead and some wounded men groaning in the road. Fearing a return of the enemy with reinforcements from LA GRENOUILLERE, Sgt. CHRISTIE took the opportunity of withdrawing, his whole party returning to our lines without a casualty. Pte FLEMING did splendid work with his bombs remaining behind with Sgt CHRISTIE to cover the retreat of the remainder.	

Summaries are contained in F. S. Regs., Part II. and the Staff Manual respectively. Title pages will be prepared in manuscript.

INTELLIGENCE SUMMARY.

(*Erase heading not required.*)

Place	Date	Hour	Summary of Events and Information	Remarks and references to Appendices
	8.10.15.		No activity today and every thing has been very quiet. weather warm.	E.A.M.
	9.10.15.		Another quiet day. An attack was expected Tonight and the men stood to till dawn. It did not materialize. The weather mild.	E.A.M.
	10.10.15.		The only unusual incident today is the appearance of a very large german flag on the ridge in front of the centre Trenches in the left half of our line. weather fine.	E.A.M.
	11.10.15		Very little activity today. Two men slightly wounded (NOS A11886 McG 73) in NO 3 or NO 4 company Trenches. weather very mild.	E.A.M.
	12.10.15		Every thing quiet today except on the hill where the enemy destroyed the CROW'S NEST with Trench mortars. (Casualties 1 killed (NO. McG 44) 2 wounded (NOS. McG 58. McG 181) weather very mild.	E.A.M.
	13.10.15		Today nothing to record. weather very mild.	E.A.M.

and the Staff Manual respectively. Title pages will be prepared in manuscript.

(Erase heading not required.)

Place	Date	Hour	Summary of Events and Information	Remarks and references to Appendices
	14.10.15		Today was featureless on the left. On the hill we were a good deal troubled by whizz bangs. Casualties 1 killed (no A10993) and 1 wounded (no 825) weather warm & bright	E.A.M.
	15.10.15		Today our artillery shelled the German trenches on the hill and stopped the whizz bangs which have been frequent up till today. Weather fine and mild.	E.A.M.
	16.10.15		Marched to Morcourt tonight after a very good relief by the Cambridgeshire Regiment, completed at 7 p.m. The battalion left the ARTILLERY DUG-OUTS about 9 p.m. and made its first halt just up the road from the FROISSY BRIDGE and the second halt at PROYARD. On arrival at MORCOURT we found MAJOR GAULT and LTS CORNISH, McDONALD, MOLSON, McKENZIE, and CURRY, who had just arrived from the base at SHORNCLIFF for duty. The march was well carried out and	

2353 Wt. W2544/1454 700,000 5/15 D. D. & L. A.D.S.S./Forms/C. 2118.

INTELLIGENCE SUMMARY.

(Erase heading not required.)

Summaries are contained in F. S. Regs., Part II. and the Staff Manual respectively. Title pages will be prepared in manuscript.

P.P.C.L.I.

Place	Date	Hour	Summary of Events and Information	Remarks and references to Appendices
			only 6 men were unable to finish with the battalion on time. A man was found drowned in the canal at FRISE today, PTE WATTERSON [illegible] ~~(No.)~~ Weather fine & cold.	E.A.M.
	17.10.15.		In billets all day. weather fine	E.A.M.
	18.10.15.		In billets all day weather fine and cold.	E.A.M.
	19.10.15.		Working parties began today Nos 1 & 2 Companies went road making at the junction of the roads between ~~Bray~~ PROYARD and MERICOURT. Nos 3 & 4 companies had battalion parade this afternoon. weather fine and cold.	E.A.M.
	20.10.15		Nos 3 & 4 companies carried on with the road building started by 1 & 2 yesterday. The battalion is standing by. weather fine and cool.	E.A.M.
	21.10.15.		In billets all day and no working parties. Weather fine and cool.	E.A.M.
	22.10.15.		Still in billets, battalion parade this afternoon,	

80

2353 Wt. W2544/1454 700,000 5/15 D. D. & L. A.D.S.S./Forms/C. 2118.

and the Staff Manual respectively. Title pages will be prepared in manuscript.

(Erase heading not required.)

Place	Date	Hour	Summary of Events and Information	Remarks and references to Appendices
	22.10.15.		LT. S.F.A. MARTIN reported back for duty today. Weather very fine.	E.A.M.
	23.10.15.		Had the battalion practising in attack this morning and remained in billets during the rest of the day. Weather fine and cold.	E.A.M.
	24.10.15.		Left MORCOURT at 8.15 a.m. and marched to BOVES. The march was well carried out and about 20 men could not finish on time, mostly on account of a new issue of boots. Route WARFUSEE-ABANCOURT VILLERS BRETONNEUX POINT 49. - POINT 60 BOVES (MAP AMIENS 12 $\frac{1}{80.000}$) Weather variable.	E.A.M.
	25.10.15.		Left BOVES this morning and marched to FERRIERES. (7.45 AM TO 12 NOON A.M.) The march was made in good order with 200 yard interval between companies and 10 yards between platoons. Route ~~CAGNY~~ CAGNY, ~~SALEUX~~, FERRIERES. Weather overcast and cold.	E.A.M.

2353 Wt. W2544/1454 700,000 5/15 D. D. & L. A.D.S.S./Forms/C. 2118.

Summaries are contained in F. S. Regs., Part II. and the Staff Manual respectively. Title pages will be prepared in manuscript.

INTELLIGENCE SUMMARY.

(Erase heading not required.)

P.P. C.L.I.

Place	Date	Hour	Summary of Events and Information	Remarks and references to Appendices
	26.10.15.		spent day in billets and apart from an escaped observation balloon which landed near our billets there is nothing of interest to record. weather very fine and cool.	E.A.M.
	27.10.15.		In billets all day, weather unsettled.	E.A.M.
	28.10.15.		In billets all day. weather rainy.	E.A.M.
	29.10.15		This morning the battalion practised an advance guard in attack. Weather very fine.	E.A.M.
	30.10.15		Today was spent in billets with company training. weather very fine	E.A.M.
	31.10.15		In billets, parade cancelled on account of weather which is rainy.	E.A.M.

10

2353 Wt. W2544/1454 700,000 5/15 D. D. & L. A.D.S.S./Forms/C. 2118.

www.ingramcontent.com/pod-product-compliance
Lightning Source LLC
Chambersburg PA
CBHW081551160426
43191CB00011B/1897
* 9 7 8 1 4 7 4 5 1 4 0 0 2 *